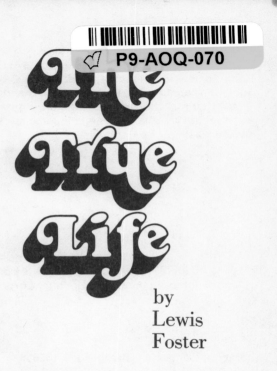

The True Life

by
Lewis
Foster

You may obtain a 64-page leader's guide and a 32-page activity book to accompany this paperback. Order numbers 1971 and 1585 from Standard Publishing or your local supplier.

New Life BOOKS™

A Division of Standard Publishing
Cincinnati, Ohio 45231

No. 40047

© 1978, the STANDARD PUBLISHING Company, a division of Standex International Corporation

Library of Congress Catalog No. 77-83656
ISBN 0-87239-192-2

Printed in U.S.A.   1978

Table of Contents

Introduction

An early Christian scholar, Clement of Alexandria, put into one word the striking characteristic of the Gospel of John. He called it the "spiritual" gospel (Eusebius, *Ecclesiastical History,* 6.14). Some have taken this to mean that the fourth Gospel is not historical. This is not true, nor was this Clement's intent. Clement was not saying that John was less historical than the other three Gospel narratives, but that they handled more the "bodily" events that could be seen. John went further to probe the significance in the spiritual realm of God's existence and the true life of man as a child of God.

When one looks into the Gospel of John, he finds the opening of the narrative goes back before the beginning of Jesus' ministry, before His beginning in Bethlehem, even before the beginning of time. "In the beginning *was* the Word . . ." Matthew and Luke begin their narratives with the birth of Jesus and the birth of John the Baptist. Mark begins with the baptism of Jesus. But John begins with the heavenly, eternal existence of the Word. This is spiritual in contrast with earthly.

John tells of a spiritual life that transcends the worldly existence of the unbeliever. Jesus has the living water that renews our souls. He has the light that drives back the darkness of ignorance, sin, and guilt. He shows the way to life, the true life, life eternal. This is life beyond the restrictions of the mere physical; it penetrates the metaphysical. It is deeper than the surface sight; it grapples with the meaning and significance of it all. To know God is life eternal (John 17:3).

For all the depth in John's treatment of Jesus' life, he used simple language and vivid, real incidents. The surface is clear, but the depths are fathomless. It has been said that the Gospel of John is like a pool where a child may wade, and an elephant can swim at the same time (cited in Leon Morris, *The Gospel According to John* [1971] p. 7). The newest Christian can gain breathtaking truths from its words, while the most advanced Biblical scholar is drawn to further studies of its passages because he knows the treasures of the fourth Gospel have never been exhausted.

The Author

In the matter of authorship one finds a similar pattern of outward appearance and then further indications just below the surface. On the surface the author does not name himself anywhere in the narrative, but just below the surface he identifies himself in a specific way. This we see in John 21:20-24.

The author was present at the last supper, so we know he was one of the twelve apostles. He refers to himself as "the disciple whom Jesus loved" and "the one who had leaned back against Jesus at the supper," so he must be one of the disciples who were very close to Jesus. Peter, James, and John were a sort of "inner circle" among the twelve (Mark 5:37; 9:2; 14:33). In John 21:20-24 it is plain that the author was not Peter, so he must be James or John. The added fact that James died very early (A.D. 44,

6

Acts 12:2) decides the question. Surely the fourth Gospel was not written that early, and so the author must be John the apostle.

This conclusion is corroborated both by indications within the Gospel itself and by the word of early Christian writers. Though it has been disputed, we see no adequate reason to doubt that John was really the author of the Gospel known by his name.

The Date

Early notices have pictured the writing of this Gospel in Ephesus toward the close of the first century. Nothing in the narrative dates the work positively. For various reasons, some students argue for an earlier date and some for a later one. However, their reasoning seems too weak to overthrow the testimony of the early writers, who date the writing of John about A.D. 90, when John was living at Ephesus.

The Setting

If this Gospel was written at the close of the first century from Ephesus, is there anything in the setting of that time and place that contributes to our understanding of the Gospel?

C.H. Dodd spends a large portion of his commentary on John in a study of Gnosticism. This Hellenistic philosophy infiltrated Christian circles and became a major problem to the church of the second century. It claimed to possess special, secret knowledge. All flesh is evil, the Gnostics said, and the spirit is good. This world is a part of the material, evil existence created by evil agents. In such a conglomeration the role of Jesus became distorted from that of the Christ proclaimed by the apostles. After treating the system at length, Dodd finally decides that actually very little Gnosticism is reflected in John. This is as it should be. John is telling us of teaching and action in Palestine in A.D. 26-30. If his writing reflected much of Ephesus at the end of the century, one might question its faithfulness to the original setting.

The Purpose

The purpose of this particular Gospel is explicitly stated. "But these are written that you may believe that Jesus is the Christ, the Son of God, and that by believing you may have life in his name" (John 20:31).

All must agree that his expressed purpose is supported by the presentation of the Gospel itself. The author lines up the testimony for Jesus page after page—who He was, what He taught, and what He did. Many suggestions are made as to more specific areas of purpose: (1) to supplement the Synoptics, giving other details and further spiritual significance, (2) to build a defense against attacks from the Jewish religious leaders, (3) to make absolutely clear that Jesus came in the flesh as a man, (4) to provide discourses and narratives appropriate for the worship of the church.

The Plan

One finds a contrast between the plan of the Synoptic Gospels and that of the Gospel of John. In the Synoptics the ministry of Jesus is almost wholly confined to Galilee, but in John a major part of Jesus' recorded work is centered in Jerusalem. Personal interviews are common in John. Claims to be the Messiah occur early in the fourth Gospel, but always to individuals, not to the crowds. The miracles recorded in John are not as numerous as those recorded in the Synoptics, but those that are included seem to be carefully chosen to serve as special signs, examples of the proof of Jesus' power and testimony to the truth of His message. He was worthy of the faith put in Him.

John's interest is not so much in chronology or geography as in the presentation of Jesus, the Son of God. Many have claimed that some of the recorded events have become displaced from the order in which the author originally placed them. Moffatt, for example, is so sure of this that in his translation of the New Testament he changes the order of the chapters in John at five different places. No textual evidence from the manuscripts supports these changes. Until there is more evidence to the contrary, it is best to follow the order of the text as it has been preserved.

The Use

This Gospel has occupied an important place in the history of the church. It was used early by Gnostic writers to claim wrongfully a support for their teaching, but it was used by orthodox fathers of the church to refute Gnostic heresies. So today it has become a center of controversy. Is the portrait of Jesus true to history or is it distorted by the beliefs of the author? The evidence indicates that it is independent, but true history.

One should approach the reading of this Gospel with a confidence established at the outset in the work of God's inspired writers and confirmed through the ages by the lives moved to accept Jesus. He is the true life and the only way. This Gospel narrative was written to lead a person to Christ, and to challenge him to further depths of spiritual truth from the first step throughout his life in the Lord.

1
When Heaven Came Down

John 1:1-18

As the curtain rises on the drama of life, two are already on stage. God and the Word are there. But it is difficult to determine whether they are two or one. The Word *(Logos)* is with God, facing toward God; and yet the Word is also God. They are not identical, but they are one. The setting is not on earth, for there is no earth. And this is not a play. This is real.

The Eternal Word

The opening verses of the Gospel of John are a formal prologue to the whole narrative that follows. They are like an explanation given by a narrator before a play. They give the setting and introduce the main character. In the description, key words are carefully chosen, words that will be important later on (e.g. life, light, witness, believe).

Who is the leading figure in this account? He is introduced as the Word (the Greek is *Logos*). After this prologue, the term is not used for Christ in the rest of the Gospel of John, nor in the rest of the New Testament except for Revelation 19:13, where "the Word of God" appears to be Christ, and 1 John 1:1, where "the Word of life" can be identified with the Son, Jesus Christ.

Logos was a term familiar to the Greek philosophers. They used it to mean "reason," frequently a reason above the reason of men, an independent force that gave order to the universe and generative power to nature. Besides "reason" it also meant "word" or "speech." John did not borrow his meaning of the word from the philosophers. He simply chose a term that people had been debating about for centuries and declared who He was and what He did. This was new to the world; it was the good news, the gospel.

These opening words of John's Gospel have the ring of the opening of Genesis, "In the beginning God created the heavens and the earth." John, however, starts with a scene before the beginning of the earth. He uses the past tense, continued action, "was," to depict the existence of the Word. Even in the beginning the Word was eternally preexistent, was distinguishable from God but had a relationship with God, and in fact the Word was God. How all this can be true at the same time is beyond the comprehension of man. If one did indeed comprehend it fully, he must be God.

Among the first of God's creative acts was to bring forth light. This was spoken into existence: "Let there be light" (Genesis 1:3). Since the *Logos* is noted as the agent through whom God made all things, it is appropriate that *Logos* be translated "Word" rather than "reason." Speech goes forth, whereas reason is confined within.

Real Life

With the presence of the Word comes life, for "in Him was life." But what is life? One can examine objects that have life, but no one has isolated life itself and put it under the microscope. One can take a synthetic grain of wheat containing all the physical ingredients of a true grain of wheat, plant it, and nothing grows. No life is implanted there. Yet some grains of wheat retrieved from the tombs of the pharaohs in Egypt have been planted after thousands of years and have grown because life was still present there. Life cannot be seen, but it is real.

There are different kinds of life. The vegetable has life, but the beast of the field has a different kind of life. Plato said, "A pig eats, sleeps, and breathes, and still remains a pig." His point was that if all a man does is eat, sleep, and breathe, then he is living the life of a pig and not of a man. Life to an intelligent being should be more than the life of a beast. The message of the Gospel of John concerns life, but the life he presents is still more than existence at the highest reaches of the mind of man. He points to the true life as a child of God.

Life is an important theme in the Gospel of John. The word is used thirty-six times in the book, more than a quarter of all the New Testament references. The kind of life offered by Jesus is the gift of God, eternal life (John 3:16). He came that men might have more abundant life (John 10:10). This new life is to know God and Jesus Christ whom He sent (John 17:3). This is what the message of the Gospel of John is about. He introduces the Word, not simply as the one who brings life, but the one in whom life itself resides. Jesus said, "I am the way, the truth, and the life" (John 14:6).

The True Light

To explain what this life is, another figure is introduced. "That life was the light of men."

Light has long been associated with understanding, enlightenment. Darkness is its opposite in ignorance and uncertainty. Light is likewise an indicator of goodness and purity, whereas evil prefers the cloak of darkness. Light is the setting for the joy and blessings of Heaven, but outer darkness describes the fate of the lost. The Word was a light-bearer ready to dispel the darkness from the lives of men. The whole of the Gospel of John tells of Christ as "the light of the world" (John 8:12). The one who follows Him will not walk in darkness, but will have the light of life. Men are urged to believe in the light (John 12:36). Just as He brought sight to the blind, He brought light to a world in darkness (John 9:5).

In mentioning the conflict between light and darkness, John uses the phrase, "but the darkness has not understood it," or as the New International Version has in a footnote, "the darkness has not overpowered it." The one Greek word can have either of these meanings, "understand" or "overpower," and it is difficult to determine which fits the context better. Perhaps John had both meanings in mind. An English word that has a similar dual meaning is "grasp." The darkness could not "grasp" the light—neither understand nor take hold of it. This is an assuring quality of light. Wherever there is light, it drives back the darkness. Darkness can never win out as long as light is there. Only when the light is removed can the darkness advance. As long as Jesus dwells in the heart of an individual, light, not darkness, prevails.

Near the first of God's creation was "Let there be light."

The Dependable Witness

Now the scene changes. We leap ahead in time from the beginnings to the century of the Gospel writer, and the point of view changes from Heaven's perspective to earth's. It seems that John the Baptist is introduced at this point for two reasons. First, the occasion of the Word's entrance into the society of people was so momentous that it required a forerunner to announce His coming, both in the happening and in John's telling of it. But a second reason is that the Gospel writer is anxious to introduce another word important to the unfolding of his account. The word is "witness" (John 1:7). John the Baptist was sent from God to give his testimony concern-

13

ing Christ. (See John 1:15 also.) John the apostle uses this word "witness" fourteen times in the Gospel, and the verb form thirty-three times. The other Gospel writers use both the noun and the verb only six times altogether. Besides John the Baptist, God bears witness to Jesus (John 5:37), the Holy Spirit testifies (John 15:26), Christ testifies of himself (John 8:14), His works give testimony (John 5:36; 10:25; 14:11), and the Scripture gives sufficient witness (John 5:39). Human witnesses also lend their voices: the disciples (John 15:27), the Samaritan woman (John 4:39), and the multitude (John 12:17).

The witness is valuable in establishing the truth. This gives strength to John's Gospel. But also this word for witness is *marturia,* which provides the basis for the English word "martyr." As a matter of fact John the Baptist did give his life in carrying out his task as a witness. Many died in those early centuries for their testimony of faith in Christ. The continuing witness today is an important part of the Christian's life. May all of us have the vigor and courage to repeat the testimony of the ancient martyrs and to be faithful even unto death.

When Heaven Came Down

"The Word became flesh and lived for a while among us" (John 1:14). This places a great gap between what John says and the musings of the philosophers and the teachings of such Jewish instructors as Philo. They had not suggested that the *Logos* became a man and lived as a human being. They had not suggested that the eternal Word was God's one and only Son and that the one true living God, who was a Spirit and could not be seen, became incarnate and lived among men. The law had been delivered through Moses, but grace and truth came through Jesus Christ.

The greatest tragedy of all is that the world did not recognize Him. His own people would not receive him. This is the same tragedy present in the world today. But there are some who do receive Him, and every one who believes in His name has the right to be born again as a child of God.

This is the prologue of John's Gospel. He is going to tell us of the true life made possible through God's one and only Son, the eternal Word.

© 1962 S.P. Co.

2
How Jesus Began

John 1:19—2:25

When Jesus began His ministry, He needed identification. But if He identified himself as the Messiah immediately, without giving instruction about what the Messiah was really like and about His kingdom, people would not find the true life. So John the Baptist acted as the announcer to identify Jesus. Then Jesus gathered His disciples to give instruction. He worked miracles as signs to authenticate His message. In this way Jesus began His ministry among His people: announcement, followers, and signs.

John the Baptist Identifies the Lamb of God

John the Baptist was the link that joined the old and the new, the prediction and its fulfillment. He himself had been predicted; for Isaiah had foretold the coming of one who would prepare the way of the Lord. And John identified himself as this voice crying in the wilderness (Isaiah 40:3).

John came to call sinners to repentance. The prophets of old had done that too, and Jesus also made it a basic note in His preaching. John was a link between the two. With the spirit and power of Elijah from the past, John preached a baptism of repentance. This baptism was a link with the future and the coming baptism in the church.

The Gospel of John does not emphasize the reforming preaching of John the Baptist as do the Synoptics (e.g. Matthew 3:7-12; Luke 3:10-18). But only the fourth Gospel tells of John the Baptist's role in identifying Jesus. John does not even tell about the baptism of Jesus, but he tells of a later time when John the Baptist spoke of the descent of the Spirit at Jesus' baptism as positive proof that Jesus was the Son of God (John 1:29-34).

At that time John pointed Jesus out as "the Lamb of God, who takes away the sin of the world" (John 1:29). This figure of the lamb was in itself a link between the past and the future. The lamb was significant in the sin sacrifices of the old covenant (Exodus 29:38-42). Especially important was the Passover lamb, both in the actual time of the exodus and in the subsequent annual remembrance of the occasion. But Jesus is our Passover lamb (1 Corinthians 5:7). Isaiah describes the suffering servant as "like a lamb that is led to slaughter" (Isaiah 53:7) . . . who "bore the sin of many" (Isaiah 53:12). Again in the book of Revelation the figure of the lamb is applied to Jesus (e.g. Revelation 5:6, 8, 13; 7:9, 10). John links the figure in the old covenant to the person and sacrifice of Christ and His eternal role in Heaven.

The Lamb provides a particularly appropriate figure. Innocence and gentleness were associated with it. But John designated Jesus "the Lamb of God." Other lambs had been offered by men, but now God had provided the Lamb, the one belonging to God. He was to provide sacrifice for the whole world.

John gave further testimony. Following his description of the descent of the Spirit upon Jesus, John stated, "I have seen and I testify that this is the Son of God." Although some manuscripts carry the reading translated "This is God's chosen One," it is more likely that "the Son of God" is what John said.

Jesus Talks With His First Disciples

What would Jesus talk about the first day He spent with two of John's disciples? One of these was Andrew (John 1:40). The other is unnamed, but he may have been John, who always avoids the use of his own name and that of his brother in his narrative. Whatever they talked about, Andrew then went to his brother, Simon, and declared, "We have found the Messiah." And after Jesus was with Philip for a time, that disciple went to Nathanael and declared they had found "the one Moses wrote about in the Law, and about whom the prophets also wrote" (John 1:45). This no doubt refers to the whole of the Old Testament Scriptures, the law and the prophets. Philip learned as did two on the way to Emmaus when the resurrected Jesus "explained to them what was said in all the Scriptures concerning himself" (Luke 24:27). This is what Jesus and His first disciples talked about in those opening days also: who the Messiah was, what He was like. And their conclusion? Jesus is the Messiah! Nathanael further concluded, "You are the Son of God; you are the King of Israel" (John 1:49).

Jesus added His own witness: "You shall all see heaven open, and the angels of God ascending and descending on the Son of Man." In other words, Jesus was providing the bridge for communication between God and man, the heavens and the earth, the spiritual and the fleshly.

Jesus Works His First Miracle

How would one begin if he had power to work miracles? He would be tempted to set up headquarters in Jerusalem or establish regular hours at an important center. But note that Jesus was attending an important social function where other people had the place of prominence: the bride and groom, the parents, the individual employed to make all the arrangements and serve as master of the feast. But this type of festival lasted about a week, and they had run out of wine. This was a little town and an unnamed family, but a need arose. This was the occasion for Jesus' first sign. It seems an unlikely time, but there was a need. Jesus' mother made the suggestion that Jesus could do something to replenish the exhausted supply of wine. His reply to her was a rebuke. He let her know that she could not run His life nor plan His schedule. Even then she alerted the servants to do anything Jesus might require of them. Did she sense that the time had come? Now Jesus added a miracle to the testimony of John the Baptist and to the convictions of the disciples He had talked to. He turned the water into wine. It is useless to debate about what kind of wine this was. The making of it was a miracle, and therefore the product was unique. The taste was better than any they had before. This is always true of the way God does things.

Jesus Indicates His Authority

After His first miracle, Jesus moved to the big cities more. Capernaum on the Sea of Galilee was important in the northern section; and Jerusalem was the center of all for the Jew. Jesus went up to the holy city for the Passover season. What He found there was cause for disappointment and anger. It was not the worship of God and the observance of His law that met the eye. There was much commercial activity accompanied by the lowing of cattle, the bleating of sheep, and the wrangling of the money changers. The temple area had become a market place, and not a very honest one at that. Edersheim estimated that the Sadducees were clearing about three hundred thousand dollars a year in their temple monopoly. Jesus would not tolerate it. Righteous indignation flashed as He drove out the oxen and sheep, freed the pigeons, and overturned the tables of the money changers.

The Synoptic Gospels do not record a cleansing of the temple this early. They describe a similar incident in the final week of Jesus' life. Some maintain that there was only one cleansing and that John has disregarded chronological order at this point. It is more likely, however, that there were two cleansings: one early and one late in His ministry. It is understandable that Synoptics do not mention this first occasion, for they tell nothing about Judean activity during His early ministry. On the other hand, if Jesus did cleanse the temple in the first year of His ministry, this explains the early and intense hostility of the religious leaders. Not only had Jesus defied their authority, but He had interfered with their money-making!

Jesus added another stone to the foundation of His claims. When He was challenged for His authority to halt the temple procedures, He boldly declared: "Destroy this temple, and I will raise it again in three days" (John 2:19). This led to further exasperation on the part of the Jewish leaders. These words of Jesus were brought up as an accusation in His trial three years later (Mark 14:57, 58). Note, however, that Jesus did not say He was going to destroy the temple. In fact, John adds the explanation: Jesus was figuratively giving a prophecy that they would destroy His temple, that is, His physical body, and three days later He would rise from the dead.

From the outset of Jesus' ministry He built upon John's testimony, instruction to His disciples, miraculous works, and declarations of authority. Our reaction today should be the same as that of the disciples: "Then they believed the Scripture and the words that Jesus had spoken" (John 2:22).

3
What Nicodemus Learned

John 3:1-36

Nicodemus came to ask a question, but he never really stated the question. Instead Jesus began to answer what was in Nicodemus' heart without waiting to hear it expressed. This relates to the closing verses of the second chapter, where we read that Jesus "knew what was in a man." Nicodemus came by night, and there was darkness over his understanding. When he departed, one does not feel that he had reached the light of noonday, but one can see the morning star rising in his heart (2 Peter 1:19). Nicodemus must wait for the unfolding of events in the three years ahead to understand the meaning of Jesus' teaching. He must hear the full gospel proclaimed and see the church established. But already the new day was dawning. His darkened understanding was exposed to the true light that enlightens every man (John 1:9). What could he learn? Nicodemus learned about the entrance to the kingdom of God. He learned about the love of God and the importance of belief. He was on the threshold of true life. It is not recorded that he entered later, but we like to think he did.

What Was the Question?

Nicodemus was a Pharisee. One can recall some of the questions the Pharisees asked on other occasions. "Is it lawful for a man to divorce his wife . . . ?" (Matthew 19:3). "Can one rightly heal on the Sabbath?" (Luke 6:7). "By what power are you, Jesus, doing these things?" (Matthew 21:23). "Why do you eat and drink with tax collectors and sinners?" (Luke 5:30). "When will the kingdom of God come?" (Luke 17:20).

Nicodemus, however, was not just an average Pharisee. He was a ruler of the Jews. Each synagogue had its rulers. But this was Jerusalem, and Nicodemus seems to have been involved with the Sanhedrin, the highest council of the Jews, numbering from seventy to a hundred members. In this case, "ruler" probably means a member of this august body, the Sanhedrin. His question may not have been the question of an ordinary Pharisee.

Moreover, Nicodemus came to Jesus by night. At least he was not trying to impress a crowd with his questions. He was not trying to trap Jesus in order to belittle Him before an audience. But why did he come by night? Was he ashamed of being seen with Jesus? Or was it because he wanted to have some privacy after the rush and turmoil of the day was over? After all, the Jews were noted for using the night for the deepest of Scripture studies. Whatever the reason for it, Nicodemus was not afraid on later occasions to stand up for Jesus, first to raise question about action to arrest Jesus (John 7:50-52), and then finally to assist Joseph of Arimathea in burying the body of Jesus. It took real courage to do that (John 19:38-42).

But what question was on his heart in this first encounter with Jesus? All one has to go on is the answer that Jesus gave. From this one must conclude that Nicodemus' unasked question had something to do with the kingdom of God. In the mind of a first-century Pharisee this phrase probably was limited by his understanding of the coming messianic age. If he had a misconception of the Messiah, his view of the kingdom would also be off the mark. In fact, Nicodemus' intended question probably had to do with both the Messiah and the kingdom, and Jesus' relationship to both.

Nicodemus Learned About the Entrance

Nicodemus began with a polite recognition that Jesus was worthy of being addressed as "Rabbi," a duly respected teacher of the Jews. He went further than this. He recognized that Jesus was a teacher come from God and could work miraculous signs. Perhaps this is what Nicodemus wanted to talk about, these signs and the coming kingdom. But Jesus swept all this aside with a warning that Nicodemus would not see the kingdom of God unless he himself was ready to enter it. He must be born *anothen.* This Greek word means either "again" or "from above." Perhaps it has both meanings here. It is obvious that Nicodemus took it to mean "again," and in a literal sense. Jesus explained further. One must be born of the water and the Spirit. If nothing more than this was said, it is doubtful that Nicodemus would have associated this new birth with Christian baptism. But John has already written of John the Baptist's baptism with water and Jesus' baptism with the Spirit (John 1:32, 33); and from the Day of Pentecost on, baptism was linked with the outward presence of water but with the indwelling gift of the Spirit (Acts 2:38). In Titus 3:5 the washing is joined to rebirth and the Spirit. One should not wonder at Jesus' giving teaching that could not be completely understood at the time it was given. The Gospel of John presents the early teaching of Jesus anticipating the Lord's Supper (John 6:53), and the people could not understand it. Here it seems that the teaching anticipated the baptism, though it would not be understood till a later time. Some deny that the passage refers to baptism. The water is interpreted as meaning physical birth. It is significant, however, that the Greek has only one preposition for both the water and the Spirit. It does not say "of the water" (one birth) and "of the Spirit" (second birth), but it says, "of the water and the Spirit" (one rebirth).

What could Nicodemus understand of this? He had started out affirming, "We know you are a teacher who has come from God"; but he ended up saying, "How can this be?" In other words, he now confessed, "I don't know." The profound truth that Jesus taught was beyond his understanding. Then Jesus gave a gentle rebuke: "You are a teacher of Israel, and you don't understand these things (concerning the Spirit)?" (John 3:10). After all, the Old Testament tells of the last days and the pouring out of God's Spirit (Isaiah 32:15; Joel 2:28, 29). It records that God said, "A new spirit will I put within you" (Ezekiel 36:26). Shouldn't a teacher of Israel be ready for additional truth about the Spirit? "We know," said Jesus, using the same expression Nicodemus had used. *"We know"* what we are talking about, but you don't believe the earthly, let alone the heavenly." (See John 3:12.) In the simple statement, "Christ died for our sins" (1 Corinthians 15:3), one sees the earthly and the heavenly. Christ died a physical death on the cross. This was the earthly. But "for our sins" transcends the physical and enters another realm. It has spiritual, heavenly consequences of an eternal nature. Even so Nicodemus was told of a rebirth of water and the Spirit. In Christian baptism the water is earthly, but the Spirit is heavenly. When Ananias told Paul, "Get up, be baptized and wash your sins away" (Acts 22:16), he spoke of the earthly (water baptism) and the heavenly (eternal spiritual consequences).

What did Nicodemus learn? He had come with a view about the kingdom of God, but it was too materialistic, too earthly. In effect, Jesus told him, "You must get turned around before you can even see the kingdom or enter it." The things of the Spirit, these are essential to the true life.

He Learned About the Love of God

From this point on (John 3:12), Nicodemus fades from the account given in the third chapter of John. The Greek manuscripts have no standard way of indicating where a quotation ends. Thus it is uncertain whether the verses 13-21 were spoken to Nicodemus, or to a wider audience on another occasion, or whether John is adding this as editorial comment. Some students end Jesus' quotation at verse 12, some at 13, some at 15, others at 21. Since the language and thought are so well knit together, it seems best to consider the whole as delivered to Nicodemus. The same thoughts may have been repeated at other times. As He moved about the country and spoke to different audiences, Jesus doubtless repeated many things over and over.

"Enter the kingdom of God" is another way of saying "have eternal life." This is why Jesus continued His instruction by speaking of necessary conditions to eternal life for the saved. First the Son of Man descends from Heaven (John 3:13). Jesus had earlier identified himself as the communicating channel between Heaven and earth (John 1:51). Then the Son of Man must be "lifted up." Later Jesus used this language again, and the meaning of it is indicated: "He said this to show the kind of death he was going to die" (John 12:33). As the children of Israel were spared in the wilderness by turning to look upon the bronze serpent held aloft in their midst (Numbers 21:8), so the sinner must look to Jesus who died on the cross for our sins. This is another condition. The sinner must look in belief to Jesus and His atoning gift.

Why has God done this? The answer is simple. God loves you so. This is one of those instances where the intellect of man is not adequate. Man cannot reason his way to establishing the love of God and the gift of His Son. Only through God's revealing himself can we be assured of this love. Accepting this in belief adds another dimension to the life of man when he finds true life as a child of God. John Calvin maintained that man can reason his way to God the Creator, but we are dependent upon revelation to know of God the Redeemer. His way of salvation is not to be searched out by the mind of man unassisted.

Nicodemus, as a Pharisee, was concerned about the minutia of the law's requirements. He wanted to know the signs of the kingdom. He wanted to know how Jesus related to all this. Jesus pointed to another of the heavenly things that Nicodemus was missing. In all the detail, one of the main points had been forgotten. God loves you. This is a message from the spiritual and is unlike the earthly. Then too, Nicodemus learned that Jesus is God's one and only Son, given to save the believers.

He Learned About the Importance of Belief

Perhaps Nicodemus was like the rich young ruler who wanted to know what he could do to inherit eternal life (Luke 18:18-25). Jesus' answer to the man of wealth was to sell all he had, give the proceeds to the poor, and then come and follow Jesus. To many, the biggest obstacle is getting rid of what separates them from God. In the rich young ruler's case it was his material wealth. But the second part is all-important: follow Jesus. In the case of Nicodemus it was not mere wealth that was his obstacle. Perhaps it was his knowledge as a Pharisee, his ties to the material world, his hopes for a material Messianic kingdom, a resistance against receiving Jesus, a reluctance to come out into the open and follow the Master. To him was given the challenge to turn to the matters of the Spirit, to know that God loved him, and to accept God's Son. "Whoever believes in him is not condemned, but whoever does not believe stands condemned already because he has not believed in the name of God's one and only Son" (John 3:18). Jesus and Nicodemus were talking together at night. Jesus warned that "men loved darkness instead of light because their deeds were evil" and that one who does evil "will not come into the light for fear that his deeds will be exposed." Jesus challenged Nicodemus to accept the Light that God had sent into the world, even God's one and only Son.

This chapter ends with another testimony from John the Baptist, but the words form a fitting summary of what Nicodemus learned: "Whoever puts his faith in the Son has eternal life, but whoever rejects the Son will not see that life, for God's wrath remains on him (John 3:36).

John Honored the Christ

More testimony is given about Jesus in John 3:22-35. He left the Jerusalem area and went into the countryside of Judea. While He and His disciples were carrying on a ministry there, John and his disciples were ministering and baptizing about thirty miles north of Jerusalem at Aenon near Salim. John continued his wholehearted support of Jesus. The friend of the bridegroom works to see that everything is prepared for the wedding, all the arrangements are made, the bride is protected, and the details are accounted for; but at the sound of the bridegroom's voice, the friend steps aside and puts everything in the hands of the one for whom all this was done. Even so John recognized that Jesus must become the center of attention, and he rejoiced to see His coming. John was only a man among men, but the Christ brought His witness from heaven. To accept Him is to gain the true life.

4
A Package of Surprises

John 4:1-42

Jesus was a package preacher. He enjoyed giving people unopened packages of truth and allowing them to discover the significance of the contents for themselves. Time after time Jesus sent an individual on his way with an armload of packages he would be struggling with the rest of his life. One such person was the Pharisee, Nicodemus. Another was the Samaritan woman.

The First Surprise: He Spoke to Her

Jesus and His disciples were returning to Galilee from Judea. They could go by any of several routes. The ordinary way for a Jew was to cross the Jordan, proceed north on the eastern side of the river, and then cross back into Galilee just south of the Sea of Galilee. This was done to avoid going through the territory of the Samaritans. The deep-seated hatred between Jews and Samaritans made it advisable to stay out of one another's reach. But in times of emergency the Jew might feel it necessary to use the short, quick route through Samaria. It still would be a three-day trip.

The Scripture says, "Now he had to go through Samaria" (John 4:4). The reason is not given. It was not a geographical necessity. There were alternate routes. Perhaps the pressure of enemies made it necessary to leave suddenly and in a certain direction. This was about the time John the Baptist was put in prison (Matthew 4:12). Or it may have been a necessity simply because it was the will of God.

While the disciples went into the town of Sychar to buy food, Jesus sat down at Jacob's well, tired at the close of a day's journey. The sixth hour probably denoted six o'clock in the evening, the way Romans indicated time. This would fit the arrival of a woman to draw her evening water.

Jesus asked her for a drink. This was the first surprise. A strange man did not speak to a strange woman. This was not the custom. But more than this, He was a Jew and she was a Samaritan. This erected a barrier that could not be ignored. Furthermore, if she drew water for Him in her jar, He would be drinking from a Samaritan receptacle, a most unusual thing for a Jew to do.

The Second Surprise: He Had Living Water

When the woman expressed her surprise that He made the request, Jesus gave her a package to puzzle over. He told her if she only realized who this was asking for water, she would be asking Him for living water.

Now what is living water? It was ordinary to refer to water of a flowing stream or spring as living water. This was in the physical realm, however, and Jesus was not speaking of that. As water is to earthly life, so this living water is to eternal life, the true life. So what is this living water? Jesus did not mean himself as the living water. He was the one who had it and could supply it. Jesus was saying that His teaching, God's revelation, was the living water that could nourish and keep alive the soul. The figure was used in the Old Testament: "All who are thirsty

29

come to the water (Isaiah 55:1); "They have forsaken me the fountain of living waters" (Jeremiah 2:13); "For as the rain comes down, and the snow from heaven," says the Lord, "so shall my word be that goes forth out of my mouth" (Isaiah 55:10, 11).

Some would press the figure farther and feel that Jesus had reference to the Holy Spirit in His words "living water." In fact, later in the Gospel of John these words of Jesus are recorded: "If a man is thirsty, let him come to me and drink. Whoever believes in me, as the Scripture has said, streams of living water will flow from within him." John adds the explanation: "By this he meant the Spirit, whom those who believed in him were later to receive. Up to that time the Spirit had not been given, since Jesus had not yet been glorified" (John 7:37-39). See also 1 Corinthians 12:13.

There is no reason why Jesus could not have referred to both the truth of His teaching and the gift of the Spirit by His figure "living water." But how much of this would the Samaritan woman understand? When she started opening the package, she looked at it in a materalistic way. She asked Jesus, "Where do you get it? How can you carry it to someone else? Are you greater than Jacob?"

Jesus helped her unwrap the package. he explained that the living water would become "a spring of water welling up to everlasting life." She decided to accept it, but still was earthbound in her concern. She would never be thirsty again; she would not have to come to this well (Jacob's) (John 4:15).

The Third Surprise: He Knew Her Past

Jesus now handed her another package. "Go, call your husband and come back." The woman decided this package was better left wrapped up. She tried to hand it back to Jesus. "I have no husband," she replied. Jesus then proceeded to unwrap the package for her. "You

30

have had five husbands, and the man you now have is not your husband."

When this was brought to light, the woman thought she had better offer a package of her own to divert attention from the subject of her husbands and her non-husband. So she introduced a subject long debated between Jews and Samaritans. Was Jerusalem or Mount Gerizim the proper place to worship God?

The Fourth Surprise: Neither Here nor There

Now it was Jesus' turn to open a package. He did not hesitate to do so, but His conclusions gave the woman another surprise. To carry out the commands of the Scriptures, the Jews maintained, a person must worship in the one true temple in Jerusalem. The Samaritans, however, maintained that Mount Gerizim, here within the sight of the Samaritan woman and Jesus, was the holy mountain. They had erected a rival temple there. It had been destroyed years before (by John Hyrcanus in 129 B.C.), but worship continued on the mountain, as it does even to this day by a people clinging to their Samaritan lineage. The Samaritan woman naturally thought that Jesus would defend the beliefs of His Jewish heritage; but He said no word for or against either Jerusalem or Gerizim, no word to settle the ancient quarrel. Instead, Jesus introduced the important point that the time was just then coming when the worship of God would not be bound to either Jerusalem or Gerizim. The sacrifice and regulations of the old covenant were of the letter and earthly; worship was to be of the spirit, that part of man that most readily responds and relates to the Spirit of God. After all, God is spirit and not flesh. On the other hand, though Jerusalem would cease to have a monopoly on worship, Jesus was not saying the Samaritans were right. They had introduced false claims and false practice. This new worship Jesus spoke of must be both in spirit and in *truth*.

31

The Fifth Surprise: Jesus Is the Messiah

The woman was not prepared to carry the subject further in this direction. She had heard the question discussed before, but not by a prophet. Still she had to try to get ahead of Jesus some way. Previously she had tried to slow Him down by asking if He was claiming to be greater than Jacob. Now it had become evident that He was some kind of prophet. So she gave Jesus one final package. The ultimate prophet would be the Messiah. Would Jesus at least admit the superiority of the Messiah? When they began opening this package, Jesus gave the Samaritan woman the greatest surprise of all. Jesus declared in effect, "I am the Messiah."

The Disciples Were Surprised

Just then His disciples returned with the provisions they had bought. Now it was the disciples' turn to be surprised. What was Jesus doing talking to this strange woman? She was a Samaritan woman at that. And one might wonder just what kind of woman she was. Yet none of the disciples dared question Jesus about her.

The disciples had another surprise. Jesus did not eat. He must have kept to himself, deep in His own thoughts. When urged to eat, He assured them He had food they did not know about. Once again the spiritual was transcending the physical. To do the will of God was His food. Could this be related to the beginning of the passage, "Now he had to go through Samaria"? It was the will of God that this Samaritan woman receive the seed of the gospel, a sip of living water, a glimpse of the true life. She in turn stirred up the whole town to come to see and hear this one who claimed to be the Messiah.

Then the disciples were surprised to see the townspeople coming out to meet Jesus. Here was a harvest that could not wait. The seed had been so recently sown, but this spiritual field was already overdue. Once more the spiritual trasncended the physical. Their crops might not be ready for four more months, but their souls were ready for harvesting that day.

Many Samaritans Believed

When the Samaritan woman left Jesus at the well the first time and went back into the town, she did not take her water jar with her. Did she forget it? Or did she leave it as a pledge to come back? In either case, the forsaken jar was a sign that she had found something more important.

John's Gospel is a report of testimonies, and the Samaritan woman gave her testimony. It was so strong that some believed because of what she told. Others came to see and hear more. Many more became believers "because of his words."

This was an exceptional occasion. Jesus gave His disciples instruction in this period to go only to the people of Israel (Matthew 10:5, 6). But it was the will of God that the seed be sown among the Samaritans; and for two days Jesus gave instruction in the heart of Samaritan land, at the foot of their holy place of worship. When Philip came preaching in Samaria over three years later (Acts 8:5), how many of his converts were people who had heard Jesus preach among them? When He was there in person many declared, "We know that this man really is the Savior of the world" (John 4:42).

5
What Kind of Proof Would It Take?

John 4:43—5:46

How can Jesus prove to a lost and dying world that He himself is the only way to true life? By affirmation He can simply declare the truth. He has the authority. But will the people listen? Will they recognize Him as God's Son? What of reason then? Can He use cold logic to lead them to the truth? Not if their feelings are strong in another direction. Can He use the testimony of others about himself and have the truth established by supporting witnesses? Not if the people refuse to believe the witnesses. Surely, then, by demonstration people can be convinced, can't they? If He can show His power by miracles, they will have to accept His message, won't they? Even so, it is possible to acknowledge the miracle on the surface, but miss the spiritual truth established in the depth. How can Jesus win people to himself, as He must do to bring new life? People come to Him by their own commitment. If a person puts his trust in Jesus, then all these proofs have their proper place and all of life begins to fall into place. Jesus is the only way to true life, but the only way to Jesus is by faith!

Unless You See Miraculous Signs . . .

Jesus' arrival in Galilee is introduced in John's Gospel by a curious combination of statements. First, notice is given that Jesus used the saying "a prophet has no honor in his own country," but in the next breath John tells that the Galileans welcomed Jesus. How are these both true, and why put them alongside one another? The key to this seeming contradiction lies in the two levels John is writing about, the earthly and the heavenly. On the surface of things Jesus was welcomed in Galilee. The people were proud and excited about the miracles He had performed in Jerusalem. How He had challenged the authorities in the temple! How He had taught the people! It was great to have a Galilean so captivating in the nation's center in Jerusalem, and Jesus received a hero's welcome as He came into Galilee. This was all on the earthly level, however. When Jesus taught of His Father, of the spiritual truths, of repentance, of love and commitment to himself, this was another matter. When it came to His deeper teaching, Jesus was rejected and without honor.

As an example of a healing miracle the story of a nobleman is given. This was a royal official, probably in the service of Herod Antipas. His home was Capernaum, but Jesus was in Cana about twenty miles away. The official had a son who was close to death; and when the father heard that Jesus was at Cana, he came to beg Him to come and heal his son.

The official had shown considerable faith by making this twenty-mile trip, and he must have been shocked at Jesus' opening statement: "Except ye see signs and wonders, ye will not believe" (John 4:48). It is significant, however, that the verbs are plural. Jesus was not speaking directly to the man; He was addressing the people. These excited, curious crowds who were welcoming Him to Galilee were looking for more miraculous signs. This is one basis for faith, but it is not the best. There are deeper levels to faith; there are deeper levels to life.

The nobleman would not allow himself to be discouraged or delayed. Again he insisted: "Sir (or Lord), come down before my child dies" (John 4:49). Jesus answered with the simple statement, "You may go. Your son will live." The man had faith based on Jesus' simple affirmation. It was not until the next day that he had confirmation of the miracle when he met his servants coming to tell him that his son's fever was gone. It had ceased at the very hour when Jesus had given His assurance to the father.

"So he and all his household believed" (John 4:53). This was a deeper faith than that which had brought the nobleman to Jesus.

Another Man Believed

The next episode takes place in Jerusalem. Some scholars complain that the Gospel of John gives evidence of having some of the material moved around from the original order of the author. They point out that Jesus is in Galilee at the close of chapter 4 and at the beginning of chapter 6, but in chapter 5 He is in Jerusalem. The proposal is made that chapter 6 should be put before chapter 5. This would make for less trips and smoother narrative. Such revisions are not supported by the manuscripts, however, nor by necessities in chronology or geography. The record as we have it simply reflects the trips Jesus was making back and forth between Galilee and Jerusalem. Furthermore, there is a way that chapter 4 relates to chapter 5. One healing resulted in the faith of a family in Galilee and another resulted in both faith and persecution in Jerusalem.

Chapter 5 records action that took place at the time of a feast of the Jews (probably the Passover) and at the pool of Bethesda at Jerusalem. Alongside the pool lay a man who had been ill for thirty-eight years. He was suffering from a type of paralysis. About him was a crowd of invalids, physically handicapped in different ways. Their belief sounds strangely like a superstition. The water of the pool was disturbed periodically, and the first one to enter the pool after this disturbance was supposed to be healed. This is what the paralytic man believed, as we see in verse 7, but he had never been able to jump in before someone else could get there before him. Notice that the Scripture does not affirm any magic healing by the pool: that is, if verse 4 is not a part of the original text. This verse explains that an angel stirred the water at times, and the first to enter the pool after this was healed of whatever ailment he had. The oldest and most trustworthy manuscripts do not include these lines, however. It is likely that some scribe wrote them in the margin to explain why the invalids were waiting by the pool. Most English translations consider this a later addition and place it in a note rather than the text. Besides its being textually unlikely and intrinsically doubtful, a natural explanation is possible. The present-day Virgin's Pool at Jerusalem is fed by underground springs that are intermittent. They flow for a time, then stop when a siphoning effect is exhausted, then start again when enough water is built up in the sources. Such action probably accounted for the occasional stirring of the water and led to an unfounded belief in an angel and healing. Naturally one who was not very sick would be able to get into the pool first, and might easily imagine he was healed.

At any rate, the paralytic was alongside the pool; he had desperate hopes but no results. Now Jesus confronted him and gave a question not hard to answer. "Do you want to get well?" The implied answer was, "Yes, but I'm not having any success." Having called attention to this, Jesus was ready to give him another solution. He said, "Get up! Pick up your mat and walk." By that command the man was challenged to put his trust in Jesus. He did so, and he was healed. In fact, Jesus issued a whole series of challenges when He told the man to pick up his mat and walk. There was a challenge to the faith of the man, both in Jesus and in his healing. There was a challenge against the oral law of the Jews, because this was the Sabbath, and the oral law forbade carrying things on that holy day. (This was set down later in the Mishnaic tractate, *Sabbath* 7.2, with implicit reference to empty beds in 10.5.) There was a challenge to the religious leaders, particularly the Pharisees, who were anxious to see that the oral law was enforced. There was a challenge to the man for obedience in response to the authority of the one in whom he had placed his trust. This was another step beyond his initial trust in Jesus. When he was halted by the Jewish authorities for carrying his mat on the Sabbath, he explained that he had been told to do so by the one who had healed him; but the former paralytic did not know his benefactor. Jesus afterward looked him up in the temple and made himself known to the healed man. This time he moved from concern for the physical to regard for the condition of the soul: "Sin no more, that nothing worse befall you."

This man then went to the authorities and told them he could now identify his healer. This need not be interpreted as betraying Jesus, as some maintain. It took courage to face the Jewish authorities again and identify the individual he had been unable to name at the first questioning. Perhaps his wish was not to betray Jesus, but rather to confess Jesus. He may have hoped the miracle would lead the authorities also to believe in the miracle worker.

The Role of the Son

The healing of the lame man at the pool of Bethesda was a link to the next episode that John records. After working this miracle on the Sabbath, Jesus was forced to defend His action. In His reply He referred to God as His Father (John 5:17), and the Jewish leaders became still more incensed, accusing Jesus of blasphemy. This presented occasion for the longest discourse of Jesus récorded up to this point in John. Earlier chapters have recorded Jesus' words on the new birth and then on the water of life, but now we see how Jesus presented the role of the Son. The Son does what God, His Father, does. Although the Sabbath was a special day, God went right on sustaining the world that day as well as other days. And the Son went on healing and doing good on the Sabbath as well as other days: He can do only what He sees His Father doing'' (John 5:19).

Jesus spoke of the love between the Father and Son (John 5:20). Because of this love and harmony, there is understanding and unity in the work that is done by both. As the Father gives life to the physically dead in a bodily resurrection, so the Son can give true life in a spiritual resurrection to those who honor Him. This true life is eternal life, and the person who believes on the Son will not be condemned. In fact, when the spiritually dead hear the voice of the Son and heed His call to believe, they cross over from death to life right now. Eternity has already begun for the dead who have been brought to the true life. And Jesus has the authority to judge. He is the Son of Man.

After this spiritual resurrection, this rebirth as one who honors the Son of Man, there will also be the resurrection from the physical graves. The good will rise to live and the evil will rise to condemnation (John 5:29).

The Call for Witnesses

Beginning in John 5:31, Jesus cites the testimony of a list of witnesses. If He makes His claims without corroboration, He says, this is not sufficient. First He appeals to ''another'' witness not named, but it seems clear as He proceeds that He refers to God himself. The Father can testify for the Son (John 5:32).

Then John the Baptist is the next witness. He was a human witness, like a lamp compared to God's sunlight (John 5:33-35).

The work that Jesus did is another witness to the truth of His message and the divinity of His person. The Father assigns that work to Him, and this is one way the Father bears witness for His Son. The Son in turn reveals the Father to His children (John 5:36-38).

The Scriptures are called to the witness stand. "You diligently study the Scriptures because you think that by them you possess eternal life. These are the Scriptures that testify about me, yet you refuse to come to me to have life" (John 5:39, 40).

Finally Moses is called as a witness to accuse those who reject Jesus. For Moses wrote of Him; and if they will not believe Moses, how will they believe what Jesus says? (John 5:45-47).

What kind of proof does it take to convince the world that God indeed became flesh and lived among us for a while in the person of His Son, Jesus Christ? The testimony is there. Man can believe in Jesus with full assurance.

6
Just a Little Boy and Jesus

John 6:1-24

This was a day to be remembered. It was filled with good news and bad news. First the good news. The disciples had just returned from an evangelistic campaign, and the successes were great. They had preached repentance, healed the sick, and driven out many demons (Mark 6:12, 13). But now the bad news. John the Baptist had been beheaded, and his disciples had buried his remains. Then they came to tell of his death, and the news reached Jesus and His disciples on this very day. They were heartbroken (Matthew 14:12, 13). In the middle of all this, Jesus said to His disciples, "Come with me by yourselves to a quiet place and get some rest" (Mark 6:31). This was a welcome invitation. The press of the crowds, exhaustion from their trip, and the weight of the tragic news of John the Baptist were taking a toll on their strength. They set out by boat across the Sea of Galilee. The next development cannot be counted all bad; for when they reached the opposite shore, they found a crowd of people already waiting for them (Mark 6:32-34). This was unfortunate in that they could not continue their solitude, but it was good in that Jesus had compassion on the people and preached the good news of the kingdom to them. But the day wore on—and there was bad news. Mealtime had long since gone by, and there was nothing to eat. This was a remote spot, and no stores were near. But then, great news! Just a little boy and Jesus were able to feed this whole multitude of five thousand men, besides the women and children (Matthew 14:21). The little boy gave all he had—five loaves and two fish—and Jesus did the rest.

Good news again. Jesus' popularity reached a climax on that day. People were so excited and drawn to the words of Jesus, so satisfied with their food, that they looked to Jesus as their hero. But bad news also. The people were so engrossed in their earthly, material desires that they failed to grasp those spiritual insights of Jesus, those challenges to live the true life as children of God. Instead they wanted to take Jesus by force and make Him a worldy king, a military conqueror.

Then good news. In the evening, Jesus thwarted the worldly plans. He went into a mountain to pray, and sent the disciples away in a boat. But the day was not over, even when darkness came. More bad news. A storm arose that threatened to swamp the disciples' boat. Then it all ended with good news. Jesus came walking on the water and took them to the opposite shore. What a day to remember!

Where and When It Happened

It was a beautiful time of the year. Wild flowers in great variety abounded on the hillsides. The rainy season was over, and the crops were ripening. People were on their way to Jerusalem for the Passover—those who were going this year. If Jesus went to Jerusalem for this Passover, there is no record of it. A year before, and two years before, He had attended. Each time great controversy had resulted, and John tells us about it. The cleansing of the temple, the challenge to Sabbath tradition, the claim that God was His Father, and a teaching that stirred hearts to repentance—these left memories one could not overlook. The law commanded that the male Jew go to Jerusalem three times each year for the main observances, and Passover was one of them. The Jews, however, had become so scattered that it was impossible for all of them to get to Jerusalem even once each year, let alone three times. Many of those living in far parts of the world counted themselves fortunate if they could return for one visit in a lifetime. Even from Galilee not everyone went each year. But what of Jesus? Was He breaking the law if He did not go? One must remember Jesus was God's Son. He fulfilled the law, but He was not subject to the law in the same way as those who were not the Son. This year He was at Capernaum when the Passover feast was about to begin. If any place could be called His home at this time, it was Capernaum.

The Sea of Galilee is about six and a half miles wide at its northern end. Jesus decided to set out with His disciples from the vicinity of Capernaum and cross eastward to the other side. But the crowds of people could see the departure and the course of the boat. The excitement was so great that they began running along the shore to keep the boat in view.

Why were the people excited? Their main interest was in the miracles of healing, the signs that He was performing. Three good results were gained. First, individuals who were healed received relief from their physical suffering. Second, this drew attention to every word Jesus spoke, to every move He made. Third, this was His opportunity to preach and to teach repentance and the coming kingdom, to present a challenge for all to put their faith in Him.

There was another reason for mounting feelings at this time. News of the death of John the Baptist fanned the smoldering coals into flame. There must have been great indignation against Herod and the Roman government that backed him. The people of Galilee always resented the foreign interlopers from Rome and hoped to see them driven out. Now, without John, their hopes for leadership focused all the more on Jesus. They were like sheep without a shepherd. They wanted Jesus to lead them.

What Was the Problem?

This was one of their problems—they needed a leader. When Jesus and His disciples landed on the opposite shore, a crowd had already gathered. They were waiting for Him. More were pouring in by the minute. The hurrying people could be seen along the shore for a long distance. And Jesus had compassion on them. He could have turned the boat southward and avoided the crowd, but He wanted to help them.

Their need went deeper than they realized. They were in their sins. They needed more than a leader; they needed a Redeemer. Jesus healed the sick, but no doubt His teaching went beyond their physical needs and penetrated to the needs of the spirit.

Several things are remarkable about this episode in the Gospel narrative. For one thing, one does not learn what Jesus taught on this occasion, but only what He did. Another interesting note is that, except for the resurrection of Jesus, this miracle alone has been recorded in all four Gospels. Is this because of its importance? It would seem from the description of Jesus' ministry in Galilee that His popularity reached a climax at this point.

A new problem emerged, however. The people had been spontaneous in leaving everything behind to gather about Jesus. He had chosen to land the boat in a remote spot with no sources of food supply. The people had been so engrossed in what was said and done that they had not noticed the passage of the day. The time had come when food was needed for physical strength to return home at the close of an eventful day. Their souls had been fed with spiritual food, but Jesus was practical and knew they were in need of physical food as well.

An Easy Answer

Jesus was not ready to provide the answer without having both His disciples and the people struggle with the problem. In putting toegether the information gained from all four Gospel narratives, it becomes clear that Jesus himself first asked the question about who was going to feed all these people. Then the disciples became disturbed and returned to put their own question to Jesus. Yes, how *were* these people going to get any food? In the meantime they had been searching throughout the crowd to see how much food was available. This increased the problem, because the minute a person was asked if he had any food with him, his immediate reaction would be to realize his hunger all the more.

It is evident that Jesus knew what He was doing from the beginning. He had deliberately steered the boat toward a remote place. He was aware of the passage of time during the day. He knew it would take hours for people to return home. He increased the apprehension by directing their attention to the need. The people, no doubt, were looking for some miraculous sign. After all, had He not changed the water into wine? Had not Moses seen to it that the people were provided manna and quail in the desert? What was going to happen here?

The answer seemed to be easy when it came. All that worry was for nothing. A little boy was found with his lunch, five barley loaves and two fish. It is inconceivable that they were taken from him against his will; rather, he must have willingly given them to Jesus.

To serve a meal to over five thousand people is no small task even with the best of facilities. How could they manage it? A bread line five thousand long would be impossible. Or if someone put out a call, "Come and get your food," there would be a stampede for the spot. Jesus had it planned. Have them seated in groups of fifties and hundreds (Mark 6:39, 40) on the spring grass. Then they can be served in an orderly way, no one will be left out, and confusion can be avoided. The disciples can see to it that each receives as much as he wants.

Where did the little boy plan to spend that day? Was he going fishing? Was he going to see a friend in a neighboring town? Was he on his way to his father's field? In any event, he decided to follow the crowd to see and hear Jesus. After hearing, he was willing to give what he had. It does not take a great person to follow Jesus, but a follower must be willing to give his all.

Jesus blessed the loaves and fish, and they were distributed to the people seated by groups on the hillside. As this was done, the supply was multiplied until all were fed. The fact that twelve baskets of fragments were taken up serves several purposes. It shows that although the supply was inexhaustible, nevertheless it was wrong to waste God's creation. Then too, it showed that everyone had enough.

Just a little boy and Jesus were able to feed the multitude. God frequently uses a seemingly small beginning to fulfill His purpose so man cannot mistake the presence of His power. Gideon started out with thirty-two thousand men, but he won the battle with only three hundred. This was "lest Israel become boastful, saying, 'My own power has delivered me'" (Judges 7:2).

False Answers

Some of the people looked beneath the surface for added meaning from this miracle and came up with false answers. Their first impression was that Jesus was the prophet who was to come into the world. This was on the right track, but they wanted to make Jesus their king. How good it would be to have a king who could provide their food every day in such an easy way, a king who could heal the sick and make whole the wounded soldiers, a king who could lead them against the legions of Rome and be victorious! They had false notions of a militant king and a materialistic kingdom.

That age had no monopoly on false answers. They are still being given today. Men still bring preconceived notions to a study of the account. Some consider it impossible that a miracle of this type could have taken place, so they try to explain away the power of Jesus. They say maybe half the people brought their own lunches, and all they did was share with one another under the influence of Jesus' preaching. Such a suggestion is far more incredible than the miracle as described. If it were true, the disciples' report would be false. They said there was no food there other than the lad's (Mark 6:38). Besides, John would be deceitful in not reporting that the people brought out their lunches later and ate them, if this is what happened. Furthermore, the reaction of the people shows they recognized that a great miracle had taken place. No sharing of lunches would have led them to such a pitch of enthusiasm. Then there were the fragments. If the people had shared their lunches, nothing would have been left over. Thus the gathering of the fragments is useful in another way—to show that the miracle really happened. Either the miracle was real, or deceit and fabrication have lined the account. We cannot believe that this story is a deceitful invention. Too many people were involved, and the accounts came from too close to the happening.

Jesus Always Makes a Way

When the people threatened to take Jesus by force and make Him king after their own notion, Jesus left the crowds and went into the mountain to pray. When they thought they had Him cornered between the sea and the mountain, He came down from the mountain in the mid-

47

dle of the night and walked on the water to reach His disciples. When the disciples were afraid of the storm and the rough sea, Jesus entered the boat and immediately they reached the other side of the sea.

7
Bread for Eternal Life

John 6:25-71

Bread and water—these are basic requirements for man's physical body. They are enough to keep a man alive. Jesus told the Samaritan woman He could provide living water forever (John 4:14); and now we see Him telling the crowds at Capernaum that He himself is the true bread for eternal life. His message sounds so simple. It deals with the basics of life, but it is difficult to understand the full meaning. In fact, the people around Jesus misunderstood Him. As Jesus answered one misunderstanding after another, He unfolded His teaching. Must we work for this bread? How do we know where to find it? How much does it cost? How can we believe this Jesus? What will happen if He is not accepted? These questions have been asked anew in each generation since that day in Capernaum.

Work for the Bread of Life

Many of the people who surrounded Jesus at this time had been present at the feeding of the five thousand. These were the men who wanted to make Him king—

their own kind of king. After the others had long since departed, they had watched for Jesus to come back down from the mountain. They thought He could not cross the sea, because there was only one boat available and He had not used that (John 6:22). All through the night they had kept their vigil. What they did not know was that Jesus walked on the water in the midst of the storm, rejoined His disciples, and arrived at the opposite shore. In the morning, some boats from Tiberias were found in the same area. Perhaps they had been forced ashore by the storm the night before. After the remnant of the crowd was satisfied that Jesus was no longer in the vicinity, they jammed the boats and went over to Capernaum. That was the most likely place to find Jesus, since it had become His headquarters. Where they located Him is uncertain. The discourse that followed ended in the synagogue, but perhaps it included several confrontations before it was completed there.

The people's first question was, "When did you get here?" One might expect them to ask, "How did you get here?" Perhaps they were disturbed at the thought of their waiting through the night for nothing if He had already made the crossing ahead of them.

At any rate, Jesus did not even answer their question, but came right to the point, just as He had done with Nicodemus. This was a situation where they should be answering to Him. The pertinent question was ,"Why are you following me?" Jesus did not even stop to ask that question, but gave the answer directly. They may have thought they were following Him to witness some miraculous sign that would indicate to them God's will and show them God's anointed one. But really they were seeking their own materialistic, selfish gain. They had received a free meal, and they were interested in enjoying many more. But this was food that would spoil. It was not what they had eaten physically the day before that was most worthwhile. It was the food having to do with the spirit and eternity. This was what the Son of Man was giving to them.

Jesus used some profoundly meaningful words to get their attention aimed in the right direction: signs, eternal life, Son of Man, God the Father, seal of approval (John 6:26, 27). Still they passed over all these, but latched on to the word "work." Indeed, Jesus had told them to work for the food that endures to eternal life. Now the men asked, "What does God want us to do? What work?"

The answer was simple, "The work of God is this: to believe in the one whom he has sent" (John 6:29).

No More Hunger

This appeal to believe prompted another question. "If you are the one sent of God, then what miraculous signs can you perform for us?" What audacity and blindness! They had just seen the feeding of the multitudes the day before. They had been seeing the healing of the sick for weeks now. Still they asked, "What sign will you perform?" Jesus did not stoop to tell them of the walking on the water.

They indicated what sign they wanted to see. After all, Moses had been responsible for bringing down manna from heaven. Now could Jesus do that? The implication was that this was a miracle greater than multiplication of loaves and fish. Jesus' reply tried to lead them a step further in their understanding. Moses had not done that, but *God* had provided the manna. Then Jesus associated himself with God in a way that Moses never did. God was Jesus' Father, and Jesus himself was the true bread that God had sent down from heaven. At this time He left His identification with the bread in the third person, but the meaning was clear. Jesus also emphasized differences between the physical manna and the true bread of God.

The people followed what He was saying up to this point. They asked that they might have this bread. In reply, Jesus changed from the third person to the first person: "I am the bread of life" (John 6:35). This is the first of the great "I am's" that Jesus spoke and John recorded in this Gospel. Six more are to come: I am the light of the world (John 8:12), the door or gate (John 10:7, 9), the good shepherd (John 10:11, 14), the resurrection and the life (John 11:25), the way, the truth, and the life (John 14:6), and the true vine (John 15:1). Each in a different figure presents the same truth. The divine "I am" of Heaven came to earth to join earthly life to the true life—the heavenly, eternal life. If a man would feed on this bread, he would never hunger again. This is the will of the Father, that through the Son and a man's belief in Him, a man will not be lost, but raised up "at the last day" (John 6:40).

The Price of True Bread

Now the crowd began to feel the pressure. They wanted to put Jesus on the spot, to make Him demonstrate His power. But they did not want to commit themselves, especially when it came to admitting that Jesus was from Heaven while all of them were from earth. After all, they had known His father and mother. At least they thought Joseph and Mary to be His parents. This does not suggest that John did not know or did not accept the account of Jesus' virgin birth as found in Matthew and Luke. All John is doing here is reporting faithfully the words of a murmuring crowd, and the doubt he expresses is theirs, not his. This record indicates that the events surrounding Jesus' birth were not common knowledge at this time, and helps to confirm the note that changing the water into wine was His first miraculous sign (John 2:11). In other words, He had grown up without any aura of the supernatural. Certainly He had been outstanding even in His childhood, but He had not been using divine powers obvious to all. Now, however, He was asking them to accept Him as descended from God, the very bread of life.

Jesus warned them to leave their doubts and stop speaking against Him. To accept Jesus is to hear the very call of God. God draws men, His Scriptures teach men (Isaiah 54:13). If an individual is standing within listening distance of God, then He will accept Jesus, and the one who believes has already begun his possession of eternal life (John 6:47). After all, those who ate the manna in the wilderness ended up in death anyway. But the one who eats of the bread of life will not die. The price of this bread is that the flesh of Jesus must be given to bring true life to the world, and the price to the individual is that he believes on Jesus. To put one's faith in Jesus included a commitment that this crowd was growing more and more reluctant to make. This commitment is marked by the eating of the bread of life.

How is this to be understood? There were religions that included in their practice the eating of raw flesh. This was extremely repulsive to think about. Furthermore, the thought of human sacrifice was horrible to the Jews and the Romans alike. In all the Roman Empire every attempt was made to stamp out any practice of human sacrifice. The Druids were the last in the first-century Roman world to be stopped. Was this the type of thing Jesus was suggesting? Surely not. More than all of this was the question of eating human flesh—this would be cannibalism. The possibility that Jesus was suggesting something along this line was revolting to the Jewish mind. If His saying could not be taken literally, was it spiritual, with no literal association at all? How could it be altogether spiritual, when He spoke of body and blood? These are certainly physical. Then was it figurative, with some kind of symbolic physical action that left the true significance in the spiritual realm? One step further, could it be sacramental in character? Augustine defined a sacrament as a "visible sign of an invisible reality." Was Jesus referring to a true channel for receiving God's saving grace?

Can You Believe?

What was the meaning? The Jews asked, "How can this man give us his flesh to eat?" (John 6:52). To the Christian who looks back on this scene from the other side of the cross, it is apparent that Jesus was giving preliminary teaching in anticipation of instituting the Lord's Supper. At the last supper He told His disciples, "Take and eat; this is my body" (Matthew 26:26), but it was the bread He passed to them. Then He took the cup and told them, "Drink from it, all of you. This is my blood of the covenant, which is poured out for many for the forgiveness of sins" (Matthew 26:27, 28), but it was the fruit of the vine that they drank.

Objections are raised that Jesus could not expect these people to understand a connection between this teaching and a sacrament that was to be established later. This is true, but Jesus was not asking them to understand. He was asking them to believe on Him. A degree of understanding must serve as a basis of belief, but greater understanding also follows belief. In the middle ages a great debate arose as to whether understanding preceded faith or vice versa. Actually it is not a question of either/or, but both/and. From a little understanding comes faith, and when one looks at things through the eyes of belief in Christ, a far greater understanding results. But this in turn leads to a greater faith, and thus the growth continues. The people in the audience at Capernaum who looked back upon these words of Jesus from a later day of faith would see more in these truths than they saw in the hour they were delivered.

Other skeptics maintain that Jesus did not have that much plan as to what He was teaching. Such teaching ahead of time would require foreknowledge of doctrine and practice still to come in the church. These modern critics say this teaching about eating Jesus' flesh was written by a later believer who simply put words into Jesus' mouth. These critics are the modern counterparts of those who left Jesus that day in Galilee. If God sent Jesus, and He taught the truths of God, He could transcend the boundaries limiting earthbound men. This too is a matter of faith.

But what would these Galileans see in these teachings if they lived before Christ's death and resurrection? One must remember that these people themselves were asking for a sign. They had introduced the example of Moses and the manna from Heaven. Jesus' sermon on the bread of life recorded here in John lies midway between the manna in the wilderness and the loaf of the Communion table. It is the connecting link. These people could have seen the connection with the past, if they had believed on Jesus, even though they could not have comprehended the connection with the future until a later time. God had provided the physical manna, and He sent the person Jesus. But Jesus was more than the manna; He was the Son of God. The manna had sustained life for a time, but then the individual had died. The Son of Man was the spiritual food that brought life everlasting. Jesus was not actual bread any more than He was an actual gate (John 10:7). Figuratively, He was bread, and they would partake of His flesh and blood. He must give himself in death, and they must give themselves in belief. Only then could this true bread bring true life.

Those Who Disbelieve

John uses different expressions to describe those who were listening to Jesus. At first, it was the "crowd" (John 6:24) who followed Him, then it was the "Jews" who began to murmur against Him (John 6:41, 52), and finally many of His "disciples" turned back and no longer followed Him (John 6:66), but "the Twelve" remained with Him. A contrast is given between Peter and Judas. One confessed Him, the other was later to betray Him. Peter's good confession at Caesarea Philippi is not recorded in John; but at this time Peter made a similar statement;

"We believe and know that you are the Holy One of God" (John 6:69). Jesus used this moment to point out the fact that He had chosen the twelve, but that one of them was a devil. The Gospel writer adds the note that this was Judas, who was to betray Him later.

Why this note of tragic betrayal, why this general desertion by the crowd and many of His disciples? What the disciples said was, "This is a hard teaching" (John 6:60). There are different ways a teaching can be hard. It may be hard to understand, or it may be difficult to accept even when understood, or it may be hard to follow after it is understood and accepted. That these people did not fully understand Jesus is evident. There was more to it, however. They were reluctant to go in the direction He was leading. He said the flesh counts for nothing, but the Spirit gives life. That day in Capernaum, many were too much conerned with fleshly, worldly things, and they turned away from Jesus. Today we face the same choice. The offer of Jesus is not to be modified. With Peter we can only say, "To whom shall we go? You have the words of eternal life" (John 6:68).

8
Jesus Faces the World

John 7:1-52

One of the hardest tasks in life is to say the right thing at the right time. Each must continually make decisions about when to talk and when not to talk. How much should one say in order to win a person? How much is just enough and not too much? How should one speak against wrong? Is it cowardly to remain silent in the presence of falsehood? Is it foolish to condemn the enemies of truth when there is little hope of converting them? What should one do when to speak will mean the loss of his physical life? Still more appalling, by remaining silent a person may put the souls of many into jeopardy for eternity. How hard it is to know just what to say! Jesus faced such decisions daily during His earthly ministry.

Ministry in Spite of Opposition

Jesus had been teaching for about two and a half years. Only half a year remained before His crucifixion. His own brothers did not believe on Him at this time. It must have been a great disappointment to God's Son to be rejected by members of His family. How could they resist His love and truth? This does not indicate any weakness of Jesus' testimony; it shows the nearsightedness, the jealousy, and the stubbornness of man's usual way. In fact, these brothers were not satisfied with refusing to accept Jesus' message and His life; they wanted to tell Him what to do. If He was truly the Messiah, why would He stay in Galilee? Go up to Jerusalem, they advised; assert your messiahship openly at the very center of Jewish activity. If Jesus would do this along with miracles to prove His claims, then perhaps His own brothers would accept His message. But Jesus chose not to make such an open declaration at this time. His brothers did not know all that was involved. If He went with them now, He would be accepting their direction. He would also be accepting publicity and fanfare as He arrived in Jerusalem with the large numbers of pilgrims going to the feast of Tabernacles. The people were watching to see if He would meet the challenge that had been issued to Him. The Jewish leaders in Jerusalem had said they would kill Him if He came within their reach. Jesus had much left to accomplish in His work. He was not ready to precipitate the final confrontation; so He said, "No, I am not going up to Jerusalem yet." This meant He was not going up with His brothers at that time in the usual manner.

What did He accomplish by refusing the invitation of His brothers? He was free to make His own plans. When He did go to Jerusalem, His appearance was unexpected. His enemies had been unable to lay plans to apprehend Him. His coming was not a spectacular entry, but a quiet appearance that enabled teaching sessions with great crowds of people. Months later, when the fullness of time had come, He did make His triumphal entry; but in that same week His death came. He was not ready for this yet, so He planned to go unobtrusively after the feast had begun.

Teaching in Spite of Disputes

Jesus arrived in Jerusalem when the week of celebration was at its height. He began teaching in the temple in the midst of those who were opposing Him, but also among many who had not heard Him before this time. They were amazed at the way He taught. He did not come as a follower of some outstanding rabbi; He had no degree from their formal educational centers. How could He speak with such authority, clarity, and challenge? Jesus answered that His teacher and authority was the one who had sent Him. This was God himself. Jesus was not seeking His own glory, and He quickly pointed out that the truth He taught was not only His, but God's. Furthermore, the threatened attacks upon Jesus were evidence that the very ones who were loudly acclaiming their loyalty to God and His law were actually rejecting God's leading as they were seeking to kill the one who was sent by God.

The crowd at the feast included Jews from foreign countries as well as those from Judea and Galilee. Many of them knew nothing of the threats against Jesus' life. They thought He must be insane to imagine such things. In answer, Jesus referred to a miracle He had worked in Jerusalem at a former feast (John 5:1-16). A lame man had been healed; but it was on the Sabbath, and bitter condemnation had followed the deed. Jesus now called attention to the fact that a baby was circumcised on the Sabbath despite the law, or rather because of the law. The law ordered circumcision on the eighth day (Leviticus 12:3), and this was considered more important than the regulations concerning work on the Sabbath. Jesus reasoned that to make a man's whole body well on the Sabbath was certainly more important also.

Jesus added the admonition to look beyond the surface appearances and exercise proper judgment. Judgment must take into account the whole man, the whole spirit of the law and its author. True judgment would take into account the depth of meaning in this miraculous sign. Not only were the limbs of a man healed, but he was made whole in spirit: a life was introduced to true life.

Claims in Spite of Denials

Now some of the people of Jerusalem had their say. It seems that three kinds of people were in Jesus' audiences on these days in the temple area. There were "the Jews," the hostile religious leaders of the Jewish people (John 7:1, 11, 13, 15). Then there were "the multitudes" of Jewish pilgrims who had come from various places to commemorate the festival. Some of these had firm opinions about Jesus; others were now hearing Him for the first time (John 7:12, 20). Finally there were the people of Jerusalem (John 7:25). These were the local crowds. They knew of the threats to stop Jesus by taking His life, but now they began to question the sincerity of such threats. Here was Jesus teaching openly in the temple area, and no apparent steps were being taken to stop Him. Did the Jewish leaders secretly feel that He really was the Messiah? Was this why they had not touched Him? But some of the people argued that Jesus could not be the Messiah, because they knew He came from Nazareth. They thought they knew all about His family and boyhood. But the Messiah—they knew He was to come from Bethlehem, of the lineage of David, but they knew nothing more about His home and origin.

As Jesus taught in the temple court, He took up this question about His origin. To make His point to the crowd of people talking among themselves, Jesus raised His voice to a shout. He agreed with the people that they knew who He was and where He was from. But once again Jesus carried His hearers below the surface facts to the more significant truths. Jesus' origin went back to the one who had sent Him. The people knew He meant God. Furthermore, He affirmed, "You do not know him, but I know him."

Jesus was never cowardly. He was willing to face the world and tell its people what they needed to hear. There were easier ways, but this was the best way. This made them think. It made them consider their own relationship with God. And if they refused to recognize Jesus for what He truly was, then this was evidence that they did not know the Father who sent Him.

Freedom in Spite of Pursuit

Some of the people believed on Jesus. They were impressed by the miraculous signs that He could perform. Others resented being told that they did not know God. They muttered darkly about laying hands on Him, perhaps to turn Him over to the authorities seeking His life, or possibly to give Him a beating themselves. When the Pharisees heard what the crowd was whispering, they decided it was time for them to make their move. They sent the temple soldiers to arrest Jesus.

Even as the soldiers came to lead Him away, Jesus declared to the people that He was going back to the one who had sent Him. Again this clearly meant God. But then Jesus went on to say that they would look for Him but would not be able to find Him, nor would they be able to follow Him where He was going. Jesus was free to go and come, to leave the world and return, but the people were confined to the world they lived in. His hearers did not want to accept this meaning. Some asked if He might be going to the Hellenistic Jews who lived in many cities around the Mediterranean.

It was the last day of the feast when Jesus stood and shouted in His deepest, loudest voice, "If you are thirsty, come to me for living water." This was the day for a priest to conduct the pouring of the water. A golden pitcher was filled with water at the pool of Siloam. The words of Isaiah 12:3 were repeated: "With joy you will draw water from the wells of salvation." Then the procession of people accompanied the priest to the temple area, where he poured the water into a vessel at the altar of burnt offering. This was done seven times on the final day of the feast. In the midst of this scene, Jesus was preaching in the temple area with bold affirmations that He could give living water, meaning the Holy Spirit. The Gospel writer explains that believers would receive this gift at a later time, after Jesus had been glorified. Perhaps the Scripture Jesus referred to was Joel 3:18: "A fountain shall come forth out of the house of the Lord."

What were the soldiers doing all this time? They were supposed to be arresting Jesus. It seems that they were enthralled along with the people. Some were saying that He was "the Prophet." Others were calling Him "the Messiah (Christ)." Still others were objecting that the Messiah would not come from Galilee. Some wanted to arrest Him, but no one dared lay a hand on Him, not even the soldiers.

Recognition in Spite of Confusion

The soldiers went back to the Jewish authorities empty-handed. Jesus had not been stopped. The angry chief priests and Pharisees demanded an explanation from the officers of the temple guard. All they could report was, "No man ever spoke like this man!" Despite the hostility and confusion, they could not help adding their testimony to the mounting recognition given to Jesus.

The Pharisees felt obligated to discredit the soldiers' reaction, so they accused them of being led astray by Jesus. Those religious leaders were wealthy. They had ample time for their religious pursuits, and many of them were born to the high status they occupied. The "multitude," the common people, were a different lot. They struggled for everything they had in life. They were not supposed to know and understand the law, but only to do what they were told was expected of them. Now the Pharisees claimed that only the lowest of the land were impressed by Jesus.

Did these leaders in the Sanhedrin know that Nicodemus had visited Jesus? One does not know. But Nicodemus heard the statement of his fellow Pharisees and could not let it pass in silence. The Pharisees said the people knew nothing of the law because they accepted Jesus as a prophet. Now Nicodemus said that those who condemned Jesus without a hearing were the ones who were violating the law. In reply, the hostile forces maintained that no prophet was to rise from Galilee. In the past the prophet Jonah had come from that region (2 Kings 14:25). Perhaps the Pharisees meant that no prophecy in Scripture predicted a prophet from Galilee in the future.

The irony of the Pharisaic insistence about the origin of Jesus lay in the fact that He did not really come from Galilee. Ultimately He did not come from Bethlehem of Judea, but from the side of God. Jesus proclaimed this in all boldness, and Nicodemus was bold enough to break his silence and at least ask a question.

Each generation sees people of the same kinds that were present that day in Jerusalem. There were those who curiously looked for the truth but never reached a conclusion: there were those who put their faith in Jesus: there were those who rejected Him: and there were those who tried to crush Him because He did not fit their plans. Jesus faced them all and spoke the truth.

9
Follow the
Light

John 8:1-30

Given the choice between light and darkness, which would you choose? No one in his right mind would choose darkness. In the darkness of Mammoth Cave, the very fish that swim in the deep, dark waters of its caverns have lost their eyesight. They are blind because there is no light.

One wants light so he can find his way. One wants light so he can see the beautiful. One needs light in order to have life.

When one looks for a figure to depict comprehension, he speaks of the light of understanding, but the darkness of ignorance. When one symbolizes goodness and purity, it is with light. When heaven is described, it is filled with light; but eternal punishment is associated with outer darkness.

The evil person desires darkness to hide his evil deeds (John 3:19). Most would like the gray at times—not light enough to show the imperfections and not dark enough to lose the way. The choice for eternity is not somewhere in between, however; it is either light or darkness.

From the opening paragraphs of the Gospel of John, Jesus was presented as the light shining in the darkness (1:4, 5). He was the light to every man; He was the true light coming into the world (1:9). In the last week of His ministry, Jesus warned the Jerusalem crowd, "You are going to have the light just a little while longer. Walk while you have the light, before darkness overtakes you. The man who walks in the dark does not know where he is going. Put your trust in the light while you have it, so that you may become sons of light" (John 12:35, 36).

Just as Jesus offered the Samaritan woman living water (John 4:10, 14), and just as He introduced the multitude along the shore of Galilee to the bread of life (John 6:51), even so He declared to the crowds in Jerusalem, "I am the light of the world. Whoever follows me will never walk in darkness, but will have the light of life" (John 8:12).

The Old Testament prophets had predicted this light. "The people who walk in darkness will see a great light; those who live in a dark land, the light will shine on them" (Isaiah 9:2; see also 10:17). These predictions penetrated still further into the future: "No longer will you have the sun for light by day, nor for brightness will the moon give you light; but you will have the Lord for an everlasting light, and your God for your glory" (Isaiah 60:19). This light is identified with God: "The Lord is my light and my salvation; whom shall I fear?" (Psalm 27:1). When Jesus claimed to be the light of the world, it was another assertion of His deity. He was the light that brings the right way into view. He was showing the way to salvation. He was driving back the darkness of sin, despair, and destruction. Life for man was a matter of following the light.

The Light Is Identified

The feast of Tabernacles was coming to its end when Jesus preached His sermon on the light of the world. Two great ceremonies associated with the feast of Tabernacles through the centuries were "the pouring out of the water" and the "temple illumination." As noted in Chapter 8, the first of these probably furnished the occasion for Jesus to call out, "If a man is thirsty, let him come to me and drink" (John 7:37). "The temple illumination" gave a similar opportunity for Him to say, "I am the light of the world." In the Court of Women were four huge golden lampstands, each with four large lamps. They were lit with great ceremony in the evening, and Edersheim says, "There was not a court in Jerusalem that was not lit up by the light" *(The Temple,* page 246). This was symbolic of the Shekinah, the radiance and glory of God's presence that once had filled His holy temple (2 Chronicles 5:14). Another light from God was recalled as the feast of Tabernacles was associated with Israel's long stay in the desert on the way to the promised land. In that period Isarael had been led by a cloud in the day but a pillar of fire by night. In the midst of the pageantry that called all this to remembrance, Jesus stood in the temple area and calmly but boldly announced to the throng, "I am the light of the world."

The Light Is Challenged

Though this talk of Jesus is usually called His sermon on the light of the world, the only reference to light is in the opening verse. In the next chapter, John records that Jesus again said, "I am the light of the world" as He gave light to a blind man (John 9:5). But here in Chapter 8 John records the sharp challenge that interrupted what Jesus was saying.

It was quite ordinary for a preacher to be interrupted by elders in the front row. They did not hesitate to question or contradict the speaker if they wished. On this occasion the Pharisees denied the claim of Jesus and demanded further proof. Jesus had cited such proof there in Jerusalem at an earlier time (John 5:31-39). He had appealed to God himself, to the Scriptures, and to the miracles He had performed. But here in Chapter 8 we see that Jesus used another approach. The questioners were demanding more testimony because they were in darkness. They did not know Jesus' origin nor His destiny. But Jesus did. He knew where He came from and where He was going. He could give reliable information about himself. But the Pharisees who challenged Him were unable to perceive the truth. Their way of judgment was distorted by selfish desires and ambitions of the flesh. Jesus did not judge anyone in the way they were judging Him. After saying all this, Jesus came again to the answer He had given before. He did not stand alone, a solitary witness about himself. God, the one who sent Him, verified all that He did and said.

A Bright Light Throws Dark Shadows

Citing the law about two witnesses, Jesus specified His Father and himself as two witnesses who spoke for Him. Then the Pharisees objected again. They said in effect, "Produce your witness. Where is your Father?"

The questioning by these Jewish leaders shows not only that they did not accept Jesus, but also that they did not understand Him and did not know God. It is quite plain that Jesus claimed God as His Father, and these men knew they could not call God before them as they would a man. Still they persisted in judging "according to the flesh" or "by human standards" (verse 15). They saw Jesus as no more than a human being; and if He had another witness, they wanted to see Him in the same way.

With verse 20 John pauses to remind us that this was taking place at the heart of the temple activity. It was at the location where the offerings were placed. Some months later, Jesus saw a widow put in her mites at this place (Mark 12:41-44). Even though the sayings of Jesus incensed the Jewish leaders, they did not dare seize Him there. The place was crowded with people, including many enthusiastic followers of Jesus who might make trouble for the police. A little earlier, police had been sent to arrest Jesus, but had come back without Him (John 7:45, 46). A little later, the leaders tried to arouse a mob to stone Him, but instead the crowd protected Him as He slipped away (John 8:59). Very briefly John explained why Jesus could remain safe in spite of the fury of the rulers: *His time had not yet come.* Willingly He would give His life six months later, but not now. So in verse 21 we see Jesus continuing His talk in the midst of His furious enemies.

Now the light cast its shadow. If they did not accept Him, they would die in their sins. At first *sin* is singular (verse 21), perhaps denoting the particular sin of rejecting Jesus. Later *sins* is plural (verse 24), for if they did not have Jesus as their Savior, all of their wrongs would need accounting for.

Who Are You, Anyway?

It seems that these people were trying to draw from Jesus a clear statement that He was divine. Then they would say He was a blasphemer. They would seize stones to stone Him, and perhaps a crowd would join them. But Jesus did not accommodate them with the excuses they wanted. All He said was, "Just what I have been claiming all along."

Then He proceeded to sum up what they should have known about Him.

1. He had much to tell them about themselves. If they would listen, He could teach them how to judge rightly rather than by faulty standards (verse 15). They needed to know right from wrong, the important from the unimportant, the spiritual from the fleshly, the believing from the unbelieving, the true from the false.

2. He was sent from God. This indicated who He was. He was the Son of Man, related to man, representative of man, the best of man all put together; but He was also the

Son of God, the representative of God bringing the truth of God. Hindered by their prejudice, His enemies did not understand this. Later He would be lifted up to die on the cross, and then lifted up to sit at the right hand of God. Then even some of His enemies would understand what He had been saying and would know it was true.

3. Furthermore, God stands with Jesus. The two are together in power and authority. And Jesus does everything to please God. There is complete harmony. Doesn't this tell us who Jesus is?

If one desires the light, he must follow the light of the world, Jesus, God's Son.

10
The Truth That Sets You Free

John 8:31-59

All of life is a quest; but what are we looking for? Is it peace? or happiness? or is it love? or freedom? None of these count for much unless they are founded on truth. But does just any truth lead one to these goals, or is it a special truth?

If ever an age deserved Paul's description of the last days, it is ours: "ever learning, and never able to come to the knowledge of the truth" (2 Timothy 3:7, King James Version). Never has man accumulated so many facts, acquired so much know-how, and penetrated so far into the nearest reaches of infinite space; but in spite of this, he has left a wide trail of confusion, uncertainty, strife, and chaos. People are maimed and destroyed in war, others intellectually set adrift without sense of direction, and others morally lost in crime and license. Man is in revolt, trying to cut all moorings to the past. Our age has turned from the desperate question of Pilate, "What is truth?" to the still more desperate question, "Is there any such thing as truth?" College freshmen are growing accustomed to hearing a cynical professor emphatically deny the existence of abiding truth and affirm that everything is relative, depending upon the time and place. This type of lecturer frequently continues by maintaining that if there were such a thing as truth it would be impossible for man to know it; and even if man were to come to a measure of the truth, it is highly unlikely that he could communicate it to another mind. Is it any wonder that the world is experiencing rebellion and chaos? The life-style of the land has been removing the pins from the hinges of truth, and the doors of knowledge are falling from their place.

Know the Truth

Jesus stood in the temple area in front of a rebellious, skeptical crowd and told them that they could indeed know the truth and that the truth would make them free. This scene is a continuation of His sermon on the light of the world, but the people He addressed at this time are described as "the Jews who had believed him." They were not His committed enemies, but neither were they His committed followers. They believed Him, but not to the extent of putting their trust in Him. Because they were not willing to obey Jesus fully, they continued to question and contradict Him.

Jesus said, "The truth will set you free." Those words are used and misused to support innumerable causes. But before one is ready to grab this statement and make use of it, he must consider the rest of the package that Jesus handed out at the same time. Before asking "what truth?" and "what freedom?" one must consider the verse that goes before: "If you hold to my teaching, you are really my disciples. Then you will know the truth, and the truth will set you free." "If you hold to my teaching!" The way to know the truth is to abide in Jesus' Word, to obey Him, truly to follow as His disciple. Not just anyone knows the truth. It is not learned in just any way, and not just any truth leads to true freedom.

In the New Testament, truth is something to be done as well as believed. "But he that doeth truth cometh to the light, that his deeds may be made manifest, that they are wrought in God (John 3:21, King James Version). When this is understood, a deeper significance is found in the words of Jesus as He prays that His followers will be sanctified in truth (John 17:17, 19). In the epistles one finds continual use of *truth* in this deeper sense. Paul warns that man exchanged the truth of God for a lie, and worshiped and served the creature rather than the Creator (Romans 1:25). In a parallel way he speaks of the truth of Christ (2 Corinthians 11:10) and the truth of the gospel (Galatians 2:5, 14; Colossians 1:5). Truth is more than God's reliability and man's consistency with the actual; truth is the revelation of God that makes known the way of salvation in Jesus Christ: "And you also were included in Christ when you heard the word of truth, the gospel of your salvation. In him, when you believed, you were marked with a seal, the promised Holy Spirit" (Ephesians 1:13). The truth is the gospel, and the gospel centers in Christ. As He is the living water who brings and sustains life, He is also the living truth that provides the way and shows the way to true life. "I am the way and the truth and the life. No one comes to the Father except through me" (John 14:6). With this meaning in view, Paul warns of the last days, which will lack a "knowledge of the truth" through rejecting God's revelation and specifically His Son Jesus Christ. It is with this meaning that John records the words of Jesus, "You will know the truth, and the truth will set you free." This is not the philosopher's truth in the concepts of men, it is not the demonstrator's cry in a civil crusade, nor is this the metaphysician's dream of an ultimate reality, nor the scientist's truth in his laboratory. This is the truth of God revealed in Jesus Christ. The freedom He brings is not the general freedom of thought or rights, but freedom from the bondage of sin and death.

All Are Slaves

One can think of many questions Jesus' hearers could have raised to gain further understanding, but they only voiced their resentment at the implication that they were slaves. They must be in bondage, according to Jesus, since He was offering to free them. To them this was outrageous. After all, they were the proud descendants of Abraham. "We . . . have never been slaves of anyone." What an absurd claim! Had they forgotten Egypt and God's deliverance from bondage? And what of their present plight? They were under the power of the Roman conqueror. They had no land they could call their own. They looked for a Messiah to deliver them; and here Jesus stood before them with an offer of freedom, and all they could do was to show their resentment!

They had missed the point again. Their worst enslavement was below the surface. "Everyone who sins is a slave to sin." This cleared up the matter of their need for freedom. But what about reference to Abraham? They said they were sons of Abraham; but Jesus was the Son of God, and here they were ready to kill Him. This did not sound like Abraham's representatives. They were taking a stand contrary to God and to Abraham. This could only associate them with the archenemy of God—the devil. He then must be their father. "Oh, no," they protested. "We are not illegitimate children. The only Father we have is God himself."

Children of the Devil

In his writing on principles of interpretation, Alexander Campbell included a section on "the listening distance." He insisted that to understand the Scriptures a person must be standing within the listening distance or he will not be able to hear the message of the Scripture. God is the center of this area, and the individual's humility is the periphery. This concept helps in understanding what Jesus said to these Jerusalem critics. They were not in listening distance. "Why is my language not clear to you? Because you are unable to hear what I say." By their rejection of Christ they were removing themselves from God's circle and joining the forces of the devil. They made him their father rather than God.

This statement from Jesus brought still further exasperation to the Jews. Angrily they said Jesus was a Samaritan and demon-possessed. Perhaps they had heard of His ministry with the Samaritans that is recorded in John 4:1-42. Perhaps they had learned that He had come through Samaria on His quick trip to arrive in the midst of this feast of Tabernacles. Perhaps they intended a slur about His obscure beginnings in Nazareth, or even a question of His birth. They may have been thinking that He did not follow all the traditions of the elders, which Samaritans also failed to follow. Or perhaps a Samaritan was the most hated being they could think of, and that was reason enough to call Jesus one.

Before Abraham Was Born, I Am

One of the most powerful statements concerning the deity of Christ was given by Jesus himself at this feast of Tabernacles. Jesus and the Jewish leaders had been having a running debate that drove them further and further apart. Jesus had promised them that if they would follow Him and keep His word, they would never die. He spoke of spiritual death. True life in Christ is eternal life with the Father. But the Jews could not see this. They knew that Abraham died, and they would not believe that anyone could be greater than Abraham. To this Jesus answered that Abraham knew of Jesus' coming and rejoiced to see His day. Does this mean that Abraham at that time of Jesus' speaking was witnessing Christ's life and rejoicing in it? Or does it mean that Abraham rejoiced in his own day because of the prospect of the coming Messiah? God had assured Abraham "In you all the families of the earth shall be blessed" (Genesis 12:3). It may be that both

74

were true: Abraham rejoiced in his day and was rejoicing now as he was aware of Jesus' work. The verb tenses are past, however, and probably the reference is to Abraham's rejoicing in his own time. The New International Version favors this interpretation, reading, "Your father Abraham rejoiced at the thought of seeing my day." But the point Jesus was making was that Abraham favored Jesus and His work, and some of these Jews were opposing Him. If they claimed Abraham as their father, they were denying their own birthright by rejecting Jesus.

This led to further ridicule from the Jews. Did Jesus really expect them to believe that He had been alive in Abraham's time or that Abraham had known Him? In all calmness and without the least egotism on the one hand or apology on the other, Jesus affirmed the plain fact that He knew to be true: "Before Abraham was born, I am."

This Gospel narrative began with a majestic declaration of the pre-existence and deity of the Word (John 1:1, 2). Now Jesus affirmed the same. By using the phrase "I am" instead of "I was," He not only claimed to have had existence in Abraham's day, but also affirmed His eternality and His deity. "I am" was the name by which God identified himself to Moses (Exodus 3:14). Now Jesus identified himself with the name of God.

The reaction of the unbelieving Jews shows that they understood this. Jesus' was claiming to be God, and to them this was blasphemy. It would have been blasphemy if the claim had not been true. Saying that it was not true, they picked up stones to kill Him. But Jesus walked from their midst as He had walked from another crowd at Nazareth under similar circumstances (Luke 4:29, 30). His time had not yet come. He was the truth, but they rejected Him. But to those who received Him and held to His teaching, then and now, it is given to know the truth and be set free.

© 1962 S.P.Co.

11
How Blind
Is Blind?

John 9:1-41

Have you read a book that has a plot within a plot? Action is going on at the same time in two different circles, and yet they are related. Have you heard a pianist play a complicated musical arrangement in which the left hand seems to be following a melody independent of the right hand, and yet the whole is one composition?

One day Jesus gave sight to a man who had been born blind. This was action enough for a thrilling story; but the account brings in another scene of action, and another type of blindness comes into view. It becomes evident that some blindness is blinder than other blindness. How blind is blind?

The Relevant Question

Some questions are relevant to every age. No question is more seriously considered than the problem of suffering. Why does a person have a handicap in life? Why is there pain? Why must hardships plague the lives of men?

No one knows just how the question came up on that day when Jesus and His disciples were passing a blind man. Probably it was not long after the feast of Tabernacles. If it happened at a different time, John may have put the account of it here because it so fittingly follows Jesus' preaching on the light of the world. We suppose the place was in or near Jerusalem, because the pool of Siloam was there. It may have been close to the temple, where the blind man could ask for offerings from the worshipers.

The Gospel says that Jesus saw the blind man, but the disciples asked the question. Did Jesus call attention to the man in such a way that the disciples were prompted to ask? Had they ever seen this blind man before? How did they know he had been blind from birth? Was the blind man aware of Jesus' preaching? How much did he know about Jesus?

These questions are not answered, but there are some probabilites. If the blind man begged daily near the temple, Jesus and the disciples probably had passed him repeatedly. Almost certainly he had heard of Jesus. "Everybody" was talking about Him as the feast of Tabernacles began (John 7:12), and interest must have grown as He taught (John 7:14, 15). The blind man may have been in the audience to hear some of His teachings. And perhaps Jesus deliberately paused near the blind man and waited for the disciples to notice him and ask the question that opened the way for more teaching and another miraculous sign.

This was the question: "Rabbi, who sinned, this man or his parents, that he was born blind?" The question of suffering is always pertinent; but, as is often the case, those asking it did not give all the alternatives. The disciples saw the problem as did the friends of Job in the Old Testament. Sin was the cause of suffering, they thought, and the worse the sin the more severe the suffering. Job had objected strenuously to that answer. He was no worse than the rest, and look at his suffering! He suggested that suffering might be a discipline to keep a person from sinning rather than a punishment because of sin. Elihu added that suffering builds character, and we may be the better for it. But at the very outset the book of Job shows another source of trouble. Satan is going up and down in the world, tempting and trying all he can. He does not test the bad ones any more than the good. Job's suffering was a test from Satan.

Jesus swept aside the disciples' suggestions. This man's sin had not made him blind, and neither had the sin of his parents. Instead of discussing the cause of blindness, Jesus focused attention on its results. Because this man was blind, the work of God was going to be displayed.

The working of God's power is associated with the presence of His Son. While He is present in the world, it is day; for He is the light of the world. He was about to give a practical demonstration of this by bringing light to a man who had lived in darkness all his life.

The Extra Test

The faith of people is constantly being tested directly or indirectly. When Jesus healed a person, He often found some way of developing or testing that person's faith. In this case, He did not need the clay, either as a medicine or as a part of some magical routine. But the clay opened the way for a command to be obeyed: "Go, wash in the pool of Siloam." It might be hard for a blind man to find his way to the pool. He might miss some contributions if he left his post. Would he have faith enough to do what Jesus said to do? Yes, he did it; and suddenly he could see!

Now an extra testing began. Even those who had known him before were uncertain of his identity. Eyesight had made a new man of him. He looked like the same man, however, and his word convinced his acquaintances that he was the same man. Then came the next question. How had he gained his sight? He gave all the credit to Jesus. He could not tell them where Jesus was now, but he knew the man called Jesus had opened his eyes.

The Convincing Sign

The testing grew more severe when the Pharisees came into the picture. Some of them pointed out that it was the Sabbath Day. Jesus could not be from God, they said. If He were, He would not have done that work on the Sabbath. Others, however, maintained that this miraculous sign could not have been done by an ordinary sinner. This must prove that Jesus had come from God and bore God's approval. As their debate grew more heated, they forced the former blind man to take a stand. What did he have to say about the one who had opened his eyes? His conclusion was that Jesus must be a prophet, a specially inspired man of God.

Since the hostile forces could make no progress in this way, they tried another tack. They said the man before them had never been blind. They said there had been no miracle. They said this man was a liar and his whole story was a fraud. Perhaps some of them really believed this. They sent for the man's parents, well knowing that ordinary citizens would be intimidated in their presence. The parents were indeed frightened, but their testimony was nevertheless a powerful bulwark of the truth. They knew the man was their son, and they knew he had been born blind. As to how he had received his sight, they were unwilling to say anything. They knew the mounting opposition to Jesus. They knew what it was like to be put out of the synagogue and suffer separation from friends and relatives. So they said, "Ask him."

Another Blindness

Finding the evidence mounting against them, the hostile Pharisees decided to end the inquiry and fall back on their own authority to keep the story of the miracle from spreading. They summoned the former blind man again. "Give glory to God," they ordered. "We know this man is a sinner." Not long before Jesus had challenged, "Can any of you prove me guilty of sin?" (John 8:46). No one had stepped forward to make accusation. Now behind His back some of the Jews were ready to declare Him a sinner because He had given sight on the Sabbath.

Obviously the man was not convinced. He would not debate about who was a sinner, but he fell back on the fact he knew: "I was blind but now I see."

At this point it seems that the Pharisees were trying to convince the man that his sight had come from God, but not from Jesus. After all, Jesus had not even been there at the pool when he had begun to see. "How did he open your eyes?"

Now the man replied with the kind of answer they deserved. He had already told them once and they did not listen. Why did they want him to tell them again? Were they thinking of becoming disciples of Jesus?

This triggered further attack, and they hurled insults at the healed man. They accused him of following Jesus, while they claimed Moses as their leader. "We know that God spoke to Moses, but as for this fellow, we don't even know where he comes from."

The former blind man turned this caustic remark into an admission of their ignorance. Their refusal to accept Jesus gave evidence of a blindness far more serious than the physical darkness experienced before by this lone defender. Could they not see that Jesus had opened his eyes? God would not give such power to a sinner. That Jesus could do this unheard of thing, opening the eyes of a man born blind, was evidence that God was with Him.

That attackers could not withstand his logic, so they threw him out of the synagogue. Jesus had declared at the beginning that this man could not be called a particulary bad sinner simply because he had suffered blindness from birth. But now the desperate attackers proclaimed him "steeped in sin" because they could not answer his arguments.

The Two Results

Jesus, hearing that the man had been put out of the synagogue, returned to ask if he believed in the Son of Man. This man did not rush into an admission without understanding, however. He in turn asked for direct information: "Who is he?" Jesus' answer was no less direct: "He is the one speaking with you." "Then the man said, 'Lord, I believe; and he worshiped him." This was one result: a man healed of physical blindness also gained the sight of Jesus as God.

The second result was that those who rejected Jesus turned out to be blind in their souls. They denied this, but in their denial of Jesus and the denial of any blindness in their lives, they became responsible for their guilt.

How blind is blind? Worst of all is the blindness that shuts out Jesus. This is far worse than a physical blindness that still allows the mind to see important truths. There are those who can see physically, but remain in sin because they are blind to Jesus. How blind is blind? If it is spiritual blindness that shuts out the Savior, it is blind as blind can be.

12
The
Shepherd
Leads

John 10:1-42

Shepherds handle their sheep in different ways. In America a shepherd usually walks behind his sheep as he drives them in the right direction. In the lands of the Bible, however, both in Bible times and now, the shepherd leads his sheep. The shepherd speaks, and the flock follows his voice. He goes ahead to show the way, to protect from dangers, to find the best in water and pasture. Another help for the sheep is the security of a fold for protection in the night, the cold, or the storm. The fold is entered by its gate, which symbolizes both the security of the fold and the freedom to leave its walls. Jesus is both our shepherd who leads us and the gate of the fold that protects us.

The Lord Is My Shepherd

The tenth chapter of John records a sermon about a shepherd, sheep, and fold. Jesus began this sermon with a type of parable. Some have said that the Gospel of John has no parables. It is true that the word used for parable in the other Gospels is not used in John, but a similar word with the same meaning is seen in John 10:6: "Jesus used this figure of speech, but they did not understand what he was telling them."

This parable began with a comparison between the shepherd who enters the fold by the gate, is respected by the watchman, and is followed by the sheep. On the other hand, the thief climbs in by another way, he is unknown to the sheep, and they run from him.

The shepherd and his sheep are an illustration of God and His people. This idea was not new to the Jews when Jesus used it. In the Psalms the Lord is the shepherd of His people Israel (Psalms 23:1; 80:1; 100:3), and also in Isaiah (40:11). False shepherds depict the false prophets leading Israel into apostasy (Ezekiel 34:2, 3; Zechariah 11:17).

If the people could understand the meaning of Jesus' figure, they would identify Jesus with the Lord and the shepherd. Those who were trying to steal the sheep, prey upon them, and lead them astray would be identified with Jesus' attackers, the chief priests and the Pharisees. Such thieves would bring death, not life.

I Shall Not Want

Jesus became more explicit when the people failed to understand. He said, "I am the gate for the sheep" (10:7). He made the promise that anyone who enters through Him will be saved. "I have come that they may have life, and have it to the full" (10:10). In contrast with the thieves who came to steal, kill, and destroy, Jesus came to bring true life. This was set down in the prologue of John's Gospel. Jesus is the source of all life, the light of man (John 1:4). Near the end of the book John states that all these things are written that men may believe that Jesus is the Christ, the Son of God and *may have life* in his name (20:31). In the closing days of His ministry, Jesus said, "I am . . . the life" (11:25; 14:6). Those who have Jesus will not lack life.

Your Rod Protects Me

Then Jesus said explicitly, "I am the good shepherd" (John 10:14). A measure of how good the shepherd is can be seen in his willingness to die on behalf of his sheep. Jesus was in fact to lay down His life for His sheep. He died in their stead, that they might have life. The contrast this time is not with the thief, but between the owner of the sheep and the hired hand who cannot be trusted when danger approaches. The good shepherd will protect his flock, even to the giving of his life.

Through the Valley of Death

Once again Jesus became more specific, more personal: "I lay down my life for the sheep" (John 10:15). He added that He had "other sheep that are not of this flock" (John 10:16). They also would listen to His voice and join His flock. There would be one flock and one shepherd. Important claims were made in this sermon. People other than Israel were to be included in the flock. Not only would Jesus lay down His life, but He would take it up again. No one would be able to take His life until He voluntarily laid it down. This was His command from His Father. His life would not end in death, but He would go through the valley and out the other side. Those who follow Him, putting their faith in the Good Shepherd, need fear no evil.

Once again the Jews were divided. Some maintained He was raving mad, driven by a demon. But there were others who insisted that no demon or person possessed by a demon ever opened the eyes of the blind.

He Restores My Soul

A new scene began at John 10:22. The feast of Dedication had arrived. This was in the month of December, and Jesus was again in the temple area speaking to the crowds. This time He was in Solomon's colonnade, where there was some protection from the cold weather.

The sermon on the Good Shepherd serves as a bridge between the discourses at the feast of Tabernacles (John 7:14—9:41) and the action described at the feast of Dedication (10:22-39). It is difficult to say just when the Good Shepherd parable was given, but the motif of the sheep continutes into this discourse at the feast of Dedication.

Some of the Jews gathered around Jesus and asked for a plain statement telling whether He was the Christ or not. This may have been intended to trap Him into making a rash statement that would get Him into trouble; but on the other hand, many people friendly to Jesus must have been wishing for a plain statement. Even John the Baptist had asked for one (Matthew 11:2, 3). Jesus had made such statements to individuals (John 4:26; 9:35, 37), but He had refrained from a public announcement that would rouse the authorities to violent moves.

In reply Jesus pointed to the miracles He had performed. These could not be denied, and they were done in His Father's name. In other words, if God was His Father, then He must be the Son.

This did not satisfy the questioners. Their trouble was that they could hear Him talking but not listen to what He was saying. His own sheep, however, hear His voice and follow Him. Those who are fully committed to Him have no doubts about who He is. These are given eternal life. ("He restores my soul.") They will never perish.

Furthermore, no one will be able to snatch them away from the hand of God (John 10:28, 29). Some would like to believe that once you have become a follower of Christ it is impossible to be lost. This verse does not say that it is impossible to run away—only that no one can come and take you away. This is a comparison of the power of God and the power of Satan or any other power opposing God. No one has the power to steal a person from the fold. One must be aware, however, that he can remove himself. Unless a person remains loyal to Christ and His teaching, he has no promise of care within the fold.

Jesus did not promise to restore souls and preserve souls by himself alone. He included God the Father in this work. Then Jesus made one of the strongest declarations of His deity that has been recorded: "I and the Father are one." Each word of this affirmation is packed with meaning: "I" (not a title such as the Son of Man, but I personally) "and the Father" (not "my Father" or some ambiguous reference) "are" (not "is": the plural verb reflects the individuality of God and Christ) "one" (not masculine in gender, but neuter, denoting one unified being rather than one person).

In the Presence of My Enemies

When Jesus said, "I and the Father are one," the Jews picked up stones to kill Him. One becomes more suspicious of the questioners now. Were they asking Him to make a plain statement so they would have an excuse to kill Him? He had come to His plain statement. He had given more than an affirmation that He was the Messiah. Jesus had made plain His claim of deity.

As the angry enemies made their move, Jesus said, "For which of the miracles do you stone me?" That stopped them for a moment. They did not want anyone to think they were killing Jesus for doing good. "Not for any of the miracles," they stormed, "but because you, a mere man, claim to be God." There was no doubt about what Jesus meant when He said He and the Father were one. They said He claimed to be God, and He did not deny it. That was exactly what He claimed.

Jesus proceeded to make an argument from the Scripture. Psalm 82:6 speaks of human judges of Israel who served as representatives of God in judgment, and it gives them the honorable titles of "gods" and "sons of the Most High." Jesus was the one God set apart and sent into the world. If those human judges could be called by such exalted names, how much more was Jesus entitled to be called the Son of God! Again He called attention to the miracles. He was doing such things as the Father does, things that only God can do. This was what He claimed to be.

Unable to answer His argument, the enemies again surged forward to seize Him, but again He escaped.

My Cup Overflows

Then Jesus left Jerusalem, where the power of His enemies was centered. It was not yet time for Him to die, so He went to the area where John had baptized in the early days. Probably former disciples of John gathered again to hear Him. They found that all John had said about this man was true. "And in that place many believed in Jesus."

The Good Shepherd was leading His sheep, and their cups were filled; but the hour was coming when the shepherd would lay down His life for His sheep.

13
Life Again

John 11:1-57

Jesus worked many miracles to prove His claim to be the Messiah, the Son of God. In writing his Gospel, John chose a series of seven miraculous signs to show how this proof was used in the ministry of Jesus. He began with changing water into wine (John 2:1-11). A nobleman's son was healed in Capernaum, though Jesus was at Cana (John 4:46-54). Later in Jerusalem, Jesus gave strength to a man who had been lame from birth (John 5:1-9). The feeding of the five thousand was a miracle so striking that all four Gospels record it (John 6:5-14). In the night that followed, Jesus came walking on the water (John 6:15-21). Again in Jerusalem Jesus gave sight to a man blind from birth (John 9:1-7). A climax was reached when Lazarus was raised from the dead (John 11:1-44).

This was a climax in several ways. Although a miracle is a miracle, and one may be just as impossible as another without the power of God, nevertheless some miracles are greater than others. To raise a man from the dead is the ultimate. Besides this, however, another crisis was at hand. The resistance of the Pharisees against

Jesus and His ministry had come to a turning point. Either they must accept Jesus for what He claimed to be, or they must retire to the sidelines and become mere spectators, or they could increase their campaign against Him to meet the mounting proof He was placing before the people. The Pharisees and chief priests chose to go all out against Christ, "so from that day on they plotted to take his life" (John 11:53). This climax of opposition brought a climax in the lives of Jesus' followers also. Was their faith strong enough to stand the test? Thomas said, "Let us also go, that we may die with Him" (John 11:15).

Many have wondered why this miracle is not recorded in the Synoptic Gospels, Matthew, Mark, and Luke, as well as in John. If it presents a climax in Jesus' ministry, they reason, it ought to be included in more than one of the records. The explanation lies in the different plans of the writers. Matthew, Mark, and Luke centered their attention on the ministry of Jesus in Galilee until they came to the events of the final week of His life. This was one way of keeping their accounts short so that more people would read them. Writing later, John apparently intended to tell some of the significant events that had been omitted. He included Jesus' early work in Judea, plus periodic activity in Jerusalem at later times. One of the events he recorded was the raising of Lazarus near Jerusalem.

Some have suggested that the raising of Lazarus did not actually happen, but that the story arose long after Jesus was gone. One should point out that resurrection miracles do appear in the Synoptics (the raising of Jairus' daughter in Mark 5:22-42, and the raising of a widow's son at Nain in Luke 7:11-15). These were important miracles also, but John does not include them because for the most part he chose material that had been omitted in the Synoptics. The minute details in John's account indicate that the record is true, the report of a reliable eyewitness.

A Friendly Family

The episode begins with the introduction of a family. There were a brother and two sisters. The brother's name was Lazarus, which is a variant form of Eleazar and means "God helps." We know nothing about him except what we learn from the Gospel of John. (There seems to be no connection between this Lazarus and the beggar with the same name who appears in Luke 16:19-31.) The two sisters were Mary and Martha. They appear also in Luke 10:38-42. It is supposed that Martha was the older, because the home is called hers and because of the responsible role she played as the hostess. But Mary won praise by her devotion to Jesus as she sat and listened to Him in their home. She is identified as the one who poured perfume on the Lord and wiped His feet with her hair (John 11:2). This incident is told in the next chapter. It seems strange to find it mentioned here before it has been recorded, but we must remember that it was well known to Christians through the records of Matthew 26:6-13 and Mark 14:3-9. Still John went on to tell about it in Chapter 12, perhaps to get the time of it on his record. It was six days before the Passover, but Matthew and Mark did not record that.

This Mary of Bethany is not to be confused with Mary Magdalene, nor Mary, the mother of James and Joseph (Matthew 27:56), nor Mary, the mother of John Mark (Acts 12:12). And of course she was not the mother of Jesus.

In the Gospel records Mary and Martha appear in three incidents: a dinner in their house (Luke 10:38-42), the raising of Lazarus (John 11:1-44), and a dinner in the house of Simon the leper (John 12:1-8; Matthew 26:6-13; Mark 14:3-9). In these accounts Martha seems to be the manager, serving the meals and attending to details of arrangement, while Mary seems to be the contemplative soul concerned with higher values than physical care and comfort.

An Appeal but No Answer

Lazarus became ill, and the sisters sent word to Jesus, "Lord, the one you love is sick." Jesus had recently left Judea after numerous attempts to arrest or kill Him (John 10:31, 39, 40). The sisters did not ask Him to come back where He would be in danger; but they knew His healing power, and it is obvious that they hoped He would save their brother's life.

Those who delivered the message must have been disappointed when Jesus made no move to help. Mary and Martha must have been even more disappointed when their messengers returned and reported that Jesus had said, "This sickness will not end in death." Perhaps Lazarus was already dead when the messengers brought back that report. What Jesus meant was that Lazarus' days on this earth were not yet over. The death he suffered was only temporary. But Jesus' hearers did not understand this. Neither did they understand what He meant when He added that Lazarus' sickness was for the glory of God and His Son.

We must not imagine that Jesus was not concerned about Lazarus and his grief-stricken sisters. To prevent such a mistaken conclusion John added, "Jesus loved Martha and her sister and Lazarus."

Then why did He wait two more days before He did anything? The reason is not given, but we can see what it probably was. Many people in Jerusalem knew Lazarus (John 11:18, 19). No doubt some of Jesus' bitter enemies knew messengers had been sent to Him. If He had gone back with the messengers, those enemies probably would have been waiting for Him, and there was no feast-day crowd to protect Him. It was not yet time for His violent death, and so He wanted to come at a time when He was not expected. The delay meant two added days of grief for the sisters, but it also meant that the resurrection miracle would be that much more irrefutable then and down through the ages.

91

Another factor may have figured in Jesus' delay of two days. The message was almost a request from a family He loved. While Jesus was often quick to respond to appeals from strangers, it is notable that He did not yield so quickly to those who were near and dear to Him. His mother once suggested that He do something about the wine supply at a wedding feast (John 2:3-11). His brothers once told Him He should go to Jerusalem to the feast of Tabernacles (John 7:3-10). In each case Jesus rebuffed the suggestion, but later did what was suggested. Since Lazarus and his family were so close to Jesus, perhaps this is another case where Jesus delayed action to make it clear that He was not subject to a schedule designed by men, even His closest friends, but only to the will of God. His compassion called for action, but wisdom and submission to God required waiting.

Lazarus Is Dead

After two days Jesus said to His disciples, "Let us go back to Judea" (11:7). This was like walking into the jaws of death. Judea was where deadly enemies were waiting for Him. Instantly the disciples protested. Jesus' enigmatic reply in John 11:9, 10 suggests that there is a favorable time for every good work, and now was the time when Jesus could make a quick trip to Bethany and get away again without falling into the fatal trap of His enemies. Thus He could continue the work He wanted to do in His day, and still postpone His death till the appointed time.

Jesus explained that Lazarus was asleep, but He was going to awaken him. In both Jewish and Greek circles sleep was used in a figurative way to mean death. But the disciples took it literally. If Lazarus had fallen into a natural sleep, they said, that was a good sign. He would get well, and there was no need for Jesus to go to Bethany. Jesus then said plainly, "Lazarus is dead . . . Let us go to him" (11:14). That was when Thomas gave his courageous and devoted words, "Let us also go, that we may die with Him" (11:16).

Disappointment but Hope

Little Bethany was full of sorrow when Jesus came. Even from Jerusalem friends had come to join the mourning. Someone saw Jesus coming and ran to tell Martha. She went to meet Him before the other mourners knew He was coming.

Her first words showed her disappointment, not only that Lazarus had died, but also that Jesus had not come sooner. Her next words, however, showed her faith and hope. Even now, she said, God would do anything Jesus asked. What could she have had in mind except renewed life for her brother?

Jesus confidently affirmed, "Your brother will rise again" (11:23). Martha's reaction to that was cautious. She was sure Lazarus would rise along with all the dead "at the last day," but surely her unspoken question must have been this: "Is that what you mean? Or are you saying he will rise again *now?*"

Jesus then delivered another "I am." Not only is He the bread of life, the light of the world, and the Good Shepherd; He is also life itself. And not only is He life, but He is the resurrection and the life: He is life in spite of death. And this life is true life. Essential to true life is belief in Jesus. Even if a believer dies, He will live forever in Christ.

Do you believe this? Jesus put the question directly to Martha, and it was a hard question. She could not understand all that Jesus meant. Her brother had believed in Jesus, and he was dead; yet Jesus said, "Whoever lives and believes in me will never die." How could that be? But Jesus did not ask if she understood; He asked if she believed, and she did. "Yes, Lord, I believe that you are the Christ, the Son of God, who was come into the world" (11:27). That covered everything. Understood or not, whatever the Christ said was true. Such was the faith of Martha.

When Mary heard that Jesus was near, she too went to meet Him. Like Martha she expressed her regret that He had not come sooner. When she and the Jews with her began to weep, Jesus wept also. "See how He loved him," they said. "Could not he who opened the eyes of the blind man have kept this man from dying?" So the stage was set for another great demonstration of what Jesus could do.

Life Again

Jesus asked where the body had been laid, and they took Him to the tomb. This was no easy moment for Jesus. Once again He was deeply moved. He ordered the stone taken from the entrance of the cave-like tomb. Practical Martha quickly objected that the odor of decomposition would fill the air, but Jesus promised that if she believed, she would see the glory of God. All might see the miracle, but only the believers would see the glory of God.

In the silence that followed His brief prayer to God, Jesus raised His voice and called for Lazarus to come from the tomb. He came out, grave clothes and all. Jesus, practical as always, ordered that he be released from the tightly wound cloth.

Fear and Plots

Jesus' coming may have taken the Pharisees by surprise, but the news reached them quickly. In great alarm they called a meeting of the Sanhedrin, the ruling council of the Jews. They had a pressing question. It was not a question of whether the miracle had happened or what it meant if it had happened. It was a question of how to stop Jesus, whoever He was and whatever He was doing. Obviously His popularity and His power with the crowds were growing. The restless people were longing for the promised Messiah, and most of them expected Him to lead them in winning freedom from the Romans who ruled over them. If Jesus would plainly and publicly announce that He was the Messiah, armed rebellion might start whether He wanted it or not. The ruling Jews realized that such a rebellion would be crushed, and those ruling Jews would be removed because they could not keep order. It was better for one man to die than to have the whole nation risk destruction. So said the high priest, and more truly than he knew he foretold what was going to happen: Jesus was going to die, not just for the Jewish nation but for all of God's people. "So from that day on they plotted to take his life" (11:53).

Withdrawn but Expected

Again their plots were frustrated as Jesus went away from Jerusalem, but the people expected Him to come to the Passover. The chief priests and Pharisees gave orders for His arrest, but still the people looked for Him. He had brought life to the physical body of Lazarus. Who could deny that He could bring life to the eternal spirits of God's people?